Scrambles & Easy Climbs in

Snowdonia

First published in 2005 by Grey Stone Books

British Library Cataloguing in Publication Data

A catalogue record of this book is available from the British Library.

ISBN 13: 978-1-902017-01-3

Conventional mapping has been based on
copyright material from The Ordnance Survey
Lic. No. 100043784

**While every effort has been taken by the authors to ensure
the accuracy of this book, changes do occur, and these may
affect the contents. Neither the author nor the publisher
accepts liability for these.**
    **It is expected that walkers and climbers, or their com-
panions, will be fully experienced in mountaincraft before
setting out on the more serious expeditions.**

Printed by Carnmor Print and Design, London Road, Preston
Repro by Forsyth & Steele, Poulton-le-Fylde, Lancashire

Scrambles & Easy Climbs in Snowdonia

Jon Sparks, Tom Hutton

& Jerry Rawson

Editor: Ronald Turnbull

Maps, sketches and line drawings by John Gillham

Grey Stone Books, Hoddlesden

Acknowledgments

The Scottish Mountaineering Club's excellent 'Skye Scrambles', compiled by Noel Williams, showed us the value of a guide which bridges the arbitrary division between scrambles and climbs. Steve Ashton's 'Scrambles in Snowdonia' really launched the whole concept of scrambling guides. The Climbers' Club has been documenting the rock-climbing in Snowdonia for almost a century. Without them, we wouldn't have known where to start.

Tom Hutton

An injured shoulder almost put paid to my involvement in this book but good friends Dafydd Davis, Rufus Duits and Gavin Rowe all had other ideas and I am eternally grateful to them for their leading prowess and, at times, their brute strength; that enabled me to get up all the routes somehow. Thanks too, to my partner Steph for accompanying me on one or two of the scrambles; I'll never forget how cool she stayed as we attempted Crib Lem in full winter conditions - it was so much easier when we went back in the summer - and for her support during the writing and editing stage. Nothing would ever get done if it weren't for two special friends, Honey and India, who get me out of bed and up into the hills every morning. Where would I be without them? And finally thanks to Jon and John for inviting to me to be part of this memorable project.

Jerry Rawson

A big thanks to all the people who have accompanied me on climbs and scrambles in Snowdonia over many years, particularly Trevor Gunner, Trevor Thatcher and Martin Trafford. Their friendship and enthusiasm, even on cold, wet days, contributed to some wonderful and memorable hill days. I also thank my wife Katie for some precious Snowdonia outings, and for her continuing support.

Jon Sparks

For Milestone Buttress Ordinary Route, 13/9/1981, I must thank Robin Taylor and Mike Thompson. Thanks, too, to all the other partners with whom I have explored the Welsh crags, notably Judith Brown. As ever, I must thank my parents for unstinting help with many aspects of my business. And above all, thanks to my partner, Bernie Carter, for sharing many of these routes, and for a million other kinds of support.

Front cover photo: On the Cneifion Arete, above Ogwen Jerry Rawson

Updates

As with all Grey Stone Books we intend to keep Scrambles and Easy Climbs in Snowdonia up to date. Visit our website for information

www.grey-stone.co.uk

Contents

Introduction

On a fine day in September 1981, three lads stood at the foot of Milestone Buttress, below the north ridge of Tryfan in the Ogwen Valley, uncoiling a fat, nearly new, orange rope, then carefully feeding it through their hands to shake out the kinks. One had a Whillans harness, its orange webbing a good match for the rope. The others tied in to simple waist-belts. Footwear was cheap canvas gym-shoes; hardware was a few slings, some hexes, and a couple of wired wedges. A copy of Blackshaw's 'Mountaineering' was in one of the rucksacks, but they had virtually memorised the key sections.

Their goal was the Ordinary Route, which, according to their borrowed, pre-metric guidebook, was 200ft high and graded Moderate. They had climbed two grades harder at V. Diff (Very Difficult) but only on a top-rope, at Warton Small Quarry in Lancashire, where none of the routes is over 35ft long.

The Milestone rock was altogether friendlier than the limestone they knew; rougher despite its polish, and warmer to the touch, it lay back at a friendlier angle. But the scale was different. At Warton they had been able to identify every hold from ground level: here whole pitches were hidden.

Each of them did some of the leading that day, taking turns to taste the special responsibility of finding the route, of placing protection and setting up belays. Since each belay was painstakingly constructed from first principles, this could take some time.

And the climb itself seemed so long, so complex. There were cracks where they learned what thrutching meant; chimneys where they could try the back-and-foot technique that they had previously only seen in the book; open edges where the ground seemed impossibly far below. And there were places where everything seemed impossible, as if they had climbed into a blind alley. But sooner or later the answer always came to light, a way that appeared to lead them out into space turning out to have holds after all.

Four and a half hours after roping up, they reached the top, a little scraped, a little tired and with a major thirst that only several pints of good Welsh bitter would assuage, but above all elated. For one in particular, that day laid the foundations of a lifelong addiction to climbing and a deep respect and affection for the Welsh mountains.

Let no-one tell you that these are mere hills. Snowdon, the Glyderau and Cadair Idris are mountains. And Milestone Buttress may be only 200ft high, but it is in the mountains and of the mountains.

And Milestone Ordinary? One of those three lads went back in 2003 to do it for this book, by which time it had been upgraded to Difficult. The rope round the waist had long since been replaced by a modern sit-harness and the gym-shoes by sticky boots. It took less than half the time and there was a lot less doubt about the outcome. If it was less of an adventure, it was even more of a pleasure. The mountains of Wales give you both.

Milestone Buttress is not typical. For there is no such a thing as a typical Welsh crag. Milestone Buttress and the Moelwynion cliffs are modest in size, clean and often sunny. Lliwedd and Craig yr Ysfa are a great deal more intimidating, sombre in atmosphere, with long and complex routes. On Lliwedd in particular, you are likely to have the buttress, if not the whole cliff, all to yourself. The isolation adds to the feeling of seriousness, compounded by imperfect rock, vegetation, and the lingering dampness. Up here, 'Wild Wales' is more than just a marketing concept. And nowhere is Wales wilder than on the Rhinogydd, where a series of short crags can be linked into an expedition whose twists and turns create a real flavour of exploration.

This book is about making the most of this huge variety. By discarding the arbitrary division between scrambling and climbing, it aims to create some particularly satisfying days on the rocks. Best of all are the ones where you can make your way from valley floor to airy windswept summit, with hands on rock wherever possible. These are the days we have called 'expeditions'. Instead of shuttling up and down the polished routes on the Idwal Slabs, strike out upward, scrambling and climbing almost all the way. Or warm up on jaunty little Bochlwyd Buttress on the way to the sterner crags of Glyder Fach; wrestle with its shady cracks and scramble on up the mini-Alpine ridges of the upper face; emerge onto the Glyder plateau in afternoon light that throws long shadows from every spiky rock. Linger for a sunset photo on the famous Cantilever; make haste carefully down the knotty ridge of the Gribin in the fading light; finally cool aching feet in the stream above Ogwen Falls.

To concentrate solely on these floor-to-ceiling linkups would be to miss out many other wonderful days, whether it's Amphitheatre Buttress - a single route that is an expedition in its own right – or the more concentrated delights of Dinas Cromlech's Flying Buttress. Here you can leave big boots and rucksacks at the foot of the climb and launch out unencumbered. There's still plenty to contend with: blind moves out of a cosy bay onto blatantly steep rock; the loneliness of belaying on a too-small ledge out of sight of your partner, with empty air nibbling at your heels and your confidence; the tilted conundrum of the final crack.

There are gentler days to be enjoyed, too; pottering about on the Moelwynion crags, for example. You could save this for when the clouds blanket the high peaks, but you don't have to. Sometimes it's nice to climb in shorts and T-shirt, and only the very hardy or the very lucky will do that on Lliwedd.

Making the Most of It
Some of these routes are possible all year round. The south-facing rock of Dinas Cromlech stays clean, dries quickly, and is rough enough to provide reasonable friction even when wet. Much the same is true of Tryfan's East Face, despite its altitude. It faces the morning sun and the aspect also offers shelter from westerly winds. However, routes on Milestone Buttress or the Idwal Slabs are very polished, which makes them slippery even when dry and doubly so when damp.

On other of the high crags, especially the north-facing ones, the rock takes longer to dry – sometimes four or five fine days are needed even in summer – and when it is wet, it's often also greasy. Add to this the discomforts of cold hands and the clumsiness of chilled limbs, and routes can become very much harder in poor conditions. As a rough rule of thumb, a route becomes one grade more difficult when wet; but shady north-facing ones may go up by two grades, occasionally more. And any exposed route becomes very much more severe in high winds. The introduction to each Expedition or Crag Day will indicate if it is particularly susceptible to bad conditions.

The climber and the environment
Climbing and scrambling bring you into close contact with the mountains, and for most people this naturally fosters appreciation and care for the mountain environment.

You may occasionally come across people, or signs, asking you to steer clear of a particular route to avoid disturbance to nesting birds. There were no known restrictions applying to any of the routes in this book in 2004, but do not assume that this will automatically be true in perpetuity, especially on more obscure crags like the Rhinogydd or Cwm Cau. It's also very rare for any such restriction to extend outside the period from February to mid-August. To be sure, and to avoid frustration on a long trip, you can check in advance. The British Mountaineering Council (BMC) website is the most comprehensive and up-to-date source of such information: click on www.thebmc.co.uk/outdoor/rad/rad.asp to go straight to the access database. Take a look at www.thebmc.co.uk/outdoor/rad/restrict.htm for more information about the whys and wherefores of nesting restrictions.

Mountain plant communities are fragile, and the inaccessibility of the crags means they are home to species long since grazed to extinction on the open slopes. Treat all vegetation with respect - what looks like a nondescript bundle of leaves may be a rare species. Stick to the rock as much as possible - it's usually pleasanter and safer anyway. Cadair Idris and the Rhinogydd lie in nature reserves. We have checked with the Countryside Council for Wales that there is no objection to climbing on the specific routes described. Anyone planning further exploration or prospecting for new routes should do the same. (Check www.ccw.gov.uk or phone 08451 306 229 to locate the appropriate area office). The CCW also asks that 'gardening' (a euphemism for the removal of vegetation) should be avoided.

On the scrambles in particular, you may encounter sheep and goats. Be aware and do not startle them. Sheep are liable to panic and may bolt in the wrong direction, possibly with disastrous results. Sheep are also perfectly capable of getting into trouble without our help. If you encounter a cragfast sheep, don't try to rescue it; give it a wide berth and report its location to a local farmer or the police when you get back to the valley. The wild goats of Snowdonia are much more crag-savvy and will usually have no difficulty getting out of your way.

Many of the problems of the wider environment are caused by the car - not just pollution and congestion, but the tearing up of verges in the demand for ever more parking spaces, and the destruction of hills to meet the demand for road-stone. Using public transport helps ease these pressures. It also means that you are freed to finish the day at a different place from where you began; you could traverse a ridge, instead of going up and down the same side. For instance, it's highly rewarding to climb by any of the three suggested itineraries to Glyder Fach, and then, instead of the rough descent back to Ogwen, enjoy an easy ridge-walk, gently descending for the most part, to Capel Curig. Other suggestions will be made in individual chapters; as services develop, further possibilities may emerge.

Public transport in the northern part of the area, around Snowdon and the Glyderau, is excellent, particularly in the summer months. The Snowdon Sherpa buses connect Llandudno, Betws y Coed, Porthmadog, Caernarfon, Rhyl and Bangor to the Ogwen, Llanberis and Gwynant valleys. The main interchange between the various services is at Pen-y-Pass.

Elsewhere in the region, services are less comprehensive. In particular it is hard to get anywhere near the Rhinogydd by public transport. The access information in each section (or under 'Ogwen Valley' for the first three sections) includes public transport details. These are based on the timetable for Summer 2004. It is always a good idea to check timetables in advance. These are normally displayed at bus stops and are readily available from tourist information centres and often at hotels and other accommodation. An invaluable booklet lists all the relevant services, both rail and bus, in Gwynedd. Details are also on the Gwynedd Council website: go to www.gwynedd.gov.uk/index.asp then follow the public transport link under 'council services'. A journey planner is at www.travelinewales.com. Some services have actually improved in recent years, and there are grounds to hope that this trend may continue.

Using this book

In the route descriptions, the directions left and right assume you are facing the rock, unless explicitly stated otherwise. However, we'll always give further clues if there's a risk of confusion.

For routes described as climbs (i.e. pitch by pitch) the overall length is the sum of the individual pitch lengths - assuming we've done our sums correctly! For scrambles we have merely given the altitude difference between bottom and top. Some of the routes involve lengthy sections of walking between steep bits, so an overall length measure is not very helpful.

For both climbs and scrambles we have given guide times. In the case of roped climbs these assume a party of two. For the scrambles the times assume you are climbing unroped. Some people like to climb fast; others like to savour every move. As long as you can finish before nightfall there's no harm in taking twice as long as our times. However people who can climb very competently on outcrops or climbing walls often find that multi-pitch routes eat up far more time than they expect. It is not a good idea to go straight from single-pitch climbs to the longest routes in this book; ease the transition with a few outings on Milestone Buttress or Clogwyn yr Oen, and then move on to the mountain crags like Tryfan or Glyder Fach.

We think the suggested Expeditions and Crag Days are elegant and satisfying combinations of routes that make for great days out. However, it is generally possible to join or leave the itinerary after any individual route, and this will be noted in the text. Over Tryfan and Glyder Fach it's even possible to mix and match routes from different itineraries. It is less easy to change your plans halfway on the single-route expeditions like Craig yr Ysfa and, especially, Lliwedd. Once committed to the route the best way out is usually to keep on climbing.

Grading: Scrambles

Scrambling guidebooks follow the 1-2-3 system, with the addition of an 'S' (for serious) to those Grade 3 routes demanding a higher level of technical ability. This system, originated by Steve Ashton in 'Scrambles in Snowdonia', seems sufficiently well-established that many people have at least a rough idea what is meant by a Grade 1 scramble, and so on.

This book will use the 1-2-3 system but without the 'S' suffix. Where a route is uncomfortably hard or exposed for a straight Grade 3 then we will grade it as a rock-climb - Moderate or even Difficult.

The best way to get the hang of any grading system is to use it. Start with Grade 1's in good conditions, and go on from there. Some people are good on slabs rather than overhangs; some are thrown by loose rock but don't mind exposure. So no grading system works exactly for everyone. And there is variation within each grade: just because you can climb one V. Diff doesn't mean you can climb them all.

Also bear in mind that the grade will increase unpredictably in poor weather. If the rock's clean and rough, a bit of wet won't make much difference, but if it's mossy or vegetated it'll be a whole new ball game. A clean but exposed ridge, on the other hand, may still be feasible in rain, but very uncomfortable in a high wind.

Very roughly, then:

Grade 1: Difficulties can normally be avoided and are not in exposed situations. Route-finding is pretty straightforward. Escape sideways is usually possible. A Grade 1 could be attempted, given good conditions, by a confident fell-walker: examples are Bristly Ridge and Llech Ddu Spur.

Grade 2: More difficult and committing situations will be found, and route-finding may require judgement. Loose rock may also require careful assessment. Inexperienced parties would carry a rope, even if it might not be used. Llechog West Rib or the Mushroom Garden are good introductions to Grade 2.

Grade 3: Can involve difficult moves, sometimes on dubious rock or in exposed situations. Route-finding may be quite complicated. A rope would be used by all but the most experienced. The Clogwyn y Person Arete is a good example.

Grading: Rock Climbs

The British grading system for rock-climbs has a long history, but can be confusing for the uninitiated.

Easy has effectively disappeared from the climbing guide books - many of those routes now appear as scrambles - so, as far as we are concerned, as with the scrambles, there are just three grades to bother about. Learn to say 'Mod', 'Diff' and 'V. Diff' if you want to sound like a climber!

Moderate: require no particular technical skill, and a beginner could expect to achieve them climbing second on the rope. They still do require proper ropework, and confidence. They can be steep, exposed and scary! The crucial pitch of Glyder Fach's Dolmen Ridge is a perfect example.

Difficult: steeper rock, smaller holds, but still within the capacity of a beginner given confidence and a good leader. Good examples are Milestone Buttress Ordinary Route and Pinnacle Rib Route on Tryfan (possibly avoiding the Yellow Slab!)

Very Difficult: Some V. Diffs involve short overhanging sections. Although these will always have good holds, they still make demands on arm strength. Others may require quite delicate climbing on small holds. Familiarity with basic technical moves such as back-and-foot and hand-jamming also helps. Routes like Kirkus's Route or Slick on Clogwyn yr Oen offer a reasonable introduction to V. Diff climbing.

We shall occasionally mention harder climbs alongside our routes. The system extends through Severe to Very Severe (VS) and then into the Extreme bracket (E1, E2, and indefinitely upwards.) If you have tackled in good style the hardest routes in this book - Flying Buttress is probably technically as hard as any, and it is certainly one of the most exposed - then a Mild Severe would be a logical next step.

Maps and Diagrams

We have included basic location and approach-route maps in addition to 3D panoramas, crag drawings and crag photographs. These should be used in conjunction with good general maps, either from the Ordnance Survey or from Harvey. Although for valley walkers the OS Explorer/Outdoor Leisure maps have the edge (they show field boundaries), for more legible crag detail and contour lines, Harvey are superior. They are also more manageable in the outdoors than the large, cumbersome, double-sided OS maps.

In their 1:25,000 Superwalker series, three titles cover the areas we ae interested in: Snowdonia the Glyderau and the Carneddau;

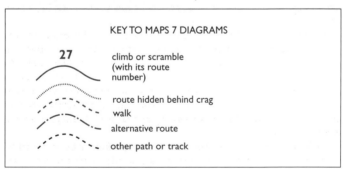

KEY TO MAPS 7 DIAGRAMS

27 climb or scramble (with its route number)

route hidden behind crag

walk

alternative route

other path or track

Snowdonia Snowdon and the Moelwynion ; Snowdonia South. See their website www.harveymaps.co.uk.

Ordnance Survey Explorer maps are the same scale and three of these cover the whole area : OL17 Snowdon/Yr Wyddfa and Conwy Valley/Dyffryn Conwy; OL18 Harlech, Porthmadog & Bala/Y Bala; OL 23 Cadair Idris & Bala Lake/Llyn Tegid. The OS website is www.ordnancesurvey.co.uk.

Getting Started

Most people move into scrambling as a natural progression from walking. Natural indeed - children are eager and uninhibited climbers, whether on wobbly bookcases, trees, or the rocks behind the beach. Unfortunately, most of us have to learn to climb all over again, much more laboriously, as adults.

Once you find that Tryfan's North Ridge and Crib Goch are enjoyable rather than terrifying, it's natural to look around for other places where you need to use hands as well as feet, where you can feel the bones of Snowdonia under your fingertips. And perhaps, as a bonus, escape the crowds.

Many people learn scrambling without ever being taught, and most of them end up as competent and safe scramblers. However, going on a course will certainly speed up this learning process, and may prevent you developing bad - and potentially dangerous - habits. See the chapter Exploring Further, at the back of the book, for more details.

Still, the time-honoured way to get scrambling is simply by going out and doing it. In this case the best advice is obvious: start with the easy stuff.

Begin, then with a Grade 1 in good conditions. The Tryfan Expedition is a good example: Tryfan's North Ridge is a great introduction, and if it was really fun, then the follow-up on Bristly Ridge is just a little bit harder. Another good one is the Llech Ddu Spur, but the difference here is that you're much more likely to be on your own. There may be odd bits of dodgy rock. You will have to decide for yourself on the safety, and possibility, of every step. It's not intrinsically any harder, but it may feel a lot more intimidating.

However accurate the guide-book's description may be, it still takes a little experience to tie it in with the mass of rock in front of you. Keep sight of the bigger picture - the overall line of the route - rather than just following the most tempting holds, which may lead into a blind alley. Such experience builds up naturally. So does the experience to spot when a particular flake of rock has worked loose, or to know whether your boot will really stick on that slab. And so, crucially, does the experience to know when to turn back, or slope off to the side. On many of the easier scrambles it's possible to escape onto easier ground without having to climb all the way back down.

Having successfully negotiated a few Grade 1's, you might move up to a Grade 2. Good 'starter' Grade 2's include the Mushroom Garden or Llechog's West Rib. You may find it equally interesting to try the Grade 1's in less good conditions.

As you move up the grades, you start to wonder about the point where the grade numbers change to mysterious adjectives like 'Mod' and 'Diff'. The difference between scrambling and climbing is not so much the routes being tackled as the way you tackle them. Climbing involves a rope, and a clearly defined route. And from ground level, that route probably looks thoroughly alarming and impossibly vertical.

Suppose, then, that you've been scrambling Grade 2 and Grade 3 and you're curious about the next step. Just what is it that you might be getting into?

Onwards and upwards

There are people who think climbing is some form of Indian Rope Trick. It isn't. In normal climbing, the aim is never to put any weight on the rope. It and all the hardware are used only for protection - not to stop you from falling off, but to stop you from hurting yourself if you do.

Rock-climbing requires a team of at least two. The route is taken in short sections called pitches, climbed in succession by the leader and then the second (or seconds: the third person up is also a 'second') while the other is firmly belayed to the rock.

Clearly the second person up isn't going to fall at all - at worst, they may swing sideways. However, the rope also secures the leader, as she places running belays at intervals for protection. These can be tape loops called slings placed over spikes of rock or threaded behind chockstones; or they can be various more technical gadgets such as nuts, with sling attached. At each of these runners the rope runs through a karabiner (a spring-loaded clip or snap-link).

With a runner in place every few metres, even if the leader does fall, she isn't going to fall far. It's not the falling that hurts, it's the stopping at the bottom - but the stretchiness of a climbing rope makes even this reasonably comfortable.

Climbing will take you onto steeper - and often cleaner - rock. You will notice more exposure - the jargon word for big drops. Climbing looks a great deal more scary than scrambling. Oddly, once you learn to have confidence in the rope, it may feel considerably less so. And provided the rope is being used properly, it is actually a great deal safer than any scramble. If you understand the principles of belaying and ropework, place secure protection, and know your own limits, then climbing on Welsh crags is a safe sport. And the mountain rescue statistics bear this out.

So what does it take to move from scrambler to rock rat?

Well, more gear, for a start. And that means not just getting the gear but learning how to use it. The legendary Joe Brown really did start off with his mother's washing line. Fortunately, however, he was soon taken in tow by climbers who knew what a real rope looked like, and how to use it. Otherwise one of the greatest of all British climbers might have had a much shorter career.

Climbing is more complex than scrambling. The quick and safe way to learn is from an experienced climber, probably on a course like those run by the National Mountaineering Centre at Plas y Brenin, Capel Curig, or through a club. An indoor climbing wall is a great place to pick up the skills of movement on rock, but won't teach you about route-finding, placing protection, or setting up safe belays. It is, however, a good way to meet people who can teach you these things. (There are more details in 'Exploring Further' at the back of the book.)

You could also learn from books (though it's beyond the scope of this one) or videos, though this is neither as effective nor as enjoyable. However good the book, a 'teach yourself' approach also entails a degree of trial and error - and the consequences of error can be dire. Many climbers - including two of the authors of this book - started this way, but we spent a lot of time top-roping on small crags before attempting to lead anything. Learning from a seasoned climber would have been both quicker and safer.

Another difference between climbing and scrambling is that climbing takes a lot longer. This is partly because only one person moves at a time, partly because of the need to place protection. There's often a third reason. The higher level of safety means that a roped climber can venture onto steeper rock, rock with fewer or smaller holds, rock where the moves are more strenuous or more intricate.

To some people this physical side is the be-all and end-all of climbing. They enjoy 'sport climbs', climbing walls, and small boulders. On our sort of climbs it is just one part - albeit an important one - of the all-round experience. Placing protection properly, both for safety and so the rope runs freely, is a gratifying skill. So is 'reading the rock', which on the larger scale helps you stay on the right route. On the smaller scale, it's surprising how often a sidestep, or just a look around, can turn an apparently impossible move into one that works and may even feel easy.

Moving up over a big drop, secure and in control, is a great feeling. So is sitting on a small ledge, feet dangling, firmly belayed, while your partner takes their turn to untangle the intricacies of a pitch. And so is arriving at the top, stepping onto level ground again as your horizon suddenly expands from a few metres of rock to distant hills and the afternoon light on the Irish Sea.

Roped scrambling

According to our earlier definition, if it's got a rope on then it's a rock-climb and so there's no such thing as roped scrambling. In fact many people will start wishing for a rope on the Grade 3 scrambles. And, of course, Grade 2 in good conditions may become very much harder in bad. If you want a rope, never be afraid to say so, even if there are others romping around quite happily unroped. It's better to be embarrassed than terrified, or injured, or dead.

A short rope (maybe 25m) will get a group out of most situations on most scrambles. While it is often possible to arrange belays with nothing more than the rope itself, it expands your options greatly if you carry a few slings and karabiners too, maybe even one or two nuts. Simply carrying the gear is no use unless at least one member of the party knows how to use it. As a minimum they should know how to tie onto the rope, how to belay from a fixed stance and how to set up a running belay. Knowledge of a simple abseil technique would be a bonus. These techniques are part of any scrambling course. These base-level skills could be acquired from a book, but must then be thoroughly practised on safe ground before they're needed.

When one member of a group is carrying a rope, it is important for all to keep in contact. It's no good one of you suddenly deciding you'd like the rope on when it's already out of sight beyond the hard bit. Of course it's even worse if you're the one out in front, you suddenly feel insecure, and the rope's with someone twenty metres below. The best person to carry the rope is the one who's least likely to need it, i.e. the most experienced member. And as a rule they should go first, but make sure they never get too far ahead.

Climbing together

Between pitched climbing and unroped climbing, there is a third way. Few British climbers, other than Alpine veterans, seem to understand anything about the art called moving together. This is a shame, because moving together, while not as safe as pitched climbing, does provide much greater security than unroped climbing, yet allows a party to move almost as fast.

Moving together has fairly limited application in Snowdonia, but is still worth knowing about. If you do have aspirations to the Alps, where reasonable speed is a crucial element in safety, it is good to get some practice in. Try it on the easier sections of Amphitheatre Buttress, for example, where it could save you a lot of time. The essence is that two (or more) climbers are roped together, but without fixed belays. A typical rope length between climbers is 15 metres or so. On easy ground you simply pick up coils of slack rope and carry them in one hand. As things get more serious, the coils are released and the leader places running belays at intervals. Sometimes a natural spike or flake of rock will act as a runner without any additional gear. The climbers continue to move together, but should not take coils in hand, and should adjust their pace to prevent any slack rope forming between them - this takes practice. If things get tougher still, it takes only moments for the second to take a secure belay and convert moving together into full-dress roped climbing.

The Ancient Art of Climbing Down

Half a century ago, down was considered as important as up. From the top of your climb, the proper thing was to descend a route of two standards easier. So after climbing Charity on Idwal Slabs (V. Diff), you might, if it wasn't too crowded, descend Ordinary Route (Mod); or after the ascent of Idwal Ordinary (Mod), the correct way down would be the Glyder Gribin (Scramble Grade 1).

For those planning to extend their rock climbing into mountaineering, being able to climb down easy rock saves abseils; saving abseils saves time and trouble and even occasionally your life. While for those planning to extend their rockclimbing into the (also rather antiquated) art of girdle traverses, down-climbing as well as sideways-climbing are called for.

But scrambling isn't necessarily about skills for somewhere else. How better to end a demanding day on Lliwedd than by slinging the rope in the sack and scrambling down the delightful easy rocks of the Snowdon Gribin? Or after the Parson's Nose, admire the sunset from the warm rocks of Crib Goch's North Ridge. Scrambling downhill has to be more fun than walking downhill. So wherever possible - and in Wales, this means quite often - we've ended our days this way.

On easy rocks, the best way to descend is facing outwards. As the ground steepens, climbing sideways gives better handhold while also allowing good view of footholds below. Where rocks are descended facing inwards, keep handholds low and body well out from the rock - which is best technique for uphill too, and looks good in the photos afterwards. When downclimbing with the rope, the second becomes the first, and accordingly takes responsibility for route-finding and the placing of protection and belays. The second will probably enjoy the added responsibility, though the leader may not agree.

Equipment
Footwear
On scrambles, it is usual to climb in the boots you have walked up in. Many people will be happy climbing Diffs and V. Diffs in boots, too. The best ones for climbing and scrambling are fairly light: it doesn't matter how good the footholds are if you can't lift your feet onto them! A good fit is essential: a boot that wobbles or flops around is uncomfortable to walk in, but dangerous for climbing. Soles should not be too bendy and should have crisp, more or less right-angled, edges. Trendy rounded bumps and knobbles are not helpful on small holds.

Ordinary trainers, with their thick spongy soles, are a poor choice for scrambling and climbing. Many people have taken to so-called approach shoes for scrambling and easy climbs. These are a cross between trainers and boots. Again, look for a good fit, reasonable support (especially lateral support) and a sensible sole.

Specialised rock boots are a pleasure to climb in. However, you can't walk up to the crag in them, and they are not essential for any of the routes in this book. Many scrambles, and a few of the climbs, involve sections of steep grass between the rocky bits. These can feel very insecure in rock-boots, especially if damp.

In damp, greasy conditions, any rubber sole can feel insecure. Bringing back nailed boots might be a good idea, except that they damage the rock. Wearing socks over the top of your boots is a time-honoured dodge that really works in these conditions. It's a lot easier to get socks over rock boots than it is to stretch them over walking boots. Wool has the best friction; synthetics like nylon are comparatively slippery - some can be worse than useless. Naturally this tactic is hard on socks. Joe Brown and chums made the first ascent of The Corner on Cloggy, when it was streaming with water and covered in muck, climbing in socks. By the top of the route all the socks were full of holes and permanently impregnated with slime, and were ceremonially interred in a small cairn, which remained in place for some years. Wool socks are not cheap, and it could be worth keeping an old pair for just this purpose.

Clothing
Whatever you wear for walking should be fine, but aim for freedom of movement - a waist-length rather than knee-length jacket, for example. Two or three thin layers are more versatile than one thick one. Scrambling, with its fairly continuous movement, will usually keep you warm. Rock-climbing, however, involves waiting around on stances. If your partner is struggling with cold fingers, these waits can get quite lengthy. You may be warm from the walk up, but you'll soon cool off. If you're going to need extra layers it's far easier to add them before you put your harness on, let alone start climbing.

Hats and gloves make a big difference, too, though if you're going to climb bare-handed - which is advisable on all but the easiest scrambles - you should let your hands acclimatise to the temperature before you start on the rock. If it's really too cold to walk up bare-handed, consider that it might be too cold to climb, unless you're walking up in frosty shade and you know that the sun will be warming the crag.

Rucksacks
Many of the trips in this book involve a linked sequence of routes. Here you will be climbing with your rucksack, rather than leaving it at the foot of the crag. If you've never climbed with a sack before, it takes a little getting used to. It helps to keep the weight to a minimum - without

omitting any essentials - and the design of the sack can also make a big difference.

Look for a slim sack, perhaps a teardrop shape which allows most of the weight to be carried low. A narrow profile at shoulder level, with straps that run fairly close to your neck rather than over the shoulder muscle, allows free arm movement. Excessively padded shoulder straps can impede movement. The ideal sack will be without side-pockets and no bigger than you need it to be. If you have to carry the rope on the outside of the sack, or even round your shoulders, for the walk up to the crag, that's a fair trade-off. Compression straps that allow you to reduce the volume of the sack will make it more stable after you've taken out the climbing gear.

The waist belt may interfere with a climbing harness. It may also get in the way when you try to make a high step up. So don't use it. But don't just leave it flapping: secure it round the back of the sack, out of the way.

Technical Gear
Climbing harnesses
Climbing harnesses do make life easier; they're convenient when belaying and give you somewhere to carry the nuts and runners. A harness becomes essential - possibly a matter of life or death - when you're on steep rock, where a fall could leave you hanging free. In such situations the traditional method of tying the rope around your waist is dangerous as the rope can ride up around your chest and cause suffocation. Even on these easier climbs and roped scrambles, unless you can be utterly certain that there's no such risk, a harness is a very good idea.

A selection of nuts is usually carried, though on the routes in this book it is unnecessary to burden yourself with micro sizes or expensive camming devices. Many modern climbers seem unable to venture out without huge 'racks' comprising every conceivable size from micro-wire to mega-Friend. The weight of that much gear can turn even the most comfortable harness into a slow-torture-belt, and searching through dozens of pieces for the right size will slow you down. Six or eight nuts are usually enough, perhaps a few more on the harder V. Diffs. What many people neglect is the value of slings. Natural protection opportunities on flakes, spikes and chockstones abound on many of the easier Welsh climbs. Modern tape slings (e.g. Spectra or Dyneema) are narrow, light and immensely strong. Four or five is not excessive. Long slings

(120cm) can always be used double to shorten them, whereas short slings can't be made longer.

Helmets
Modern helmets are lighter, more comfortable and better-looking than ever before. There's little excuse for not wearing one wherever there's a risk either of falling off or of anything (or anybody!) falling from above. This includes the steeper scrambles, where loose rocks are a possibility, as well as rock climbs. The danger of things being knocked off or dropped from above is greater when there are others on the route ahead of you, be they climbers, cragfast sheep or wild goats.

A cautionary note

Of course, the descriptions and diagrams in this book are as clear as they can possibly be, but experience still helps in reading the rock. The introduction to each route will point out routes which are more than usually devious, where protection is less than generous, or stances less than large, but you need to be able to interpret this information in accordance with your own ability and experience and the conditions on the day.

Guidebooks sometimes refer to rock being 'perfect', 'impeccable' and so on. Sadly nothing in life is perfect, not even the Idwal Slabs. Much of the rock in Snowdonia is superb, but occasional loose holds occur even on well-used routes. Learn to assess the rock first visually and then by testing suspect holds before committing to them. Some holds will actually move, others will sound hollow when tapped.

If rock does seem loose, distribute your weight. The traditional advice is to maintain three points of contact but this should really be three points of support. Sometimes holds that won't stand a direct pull can be pushed instead.

In some senses, the harder scrambles can actually be harder than the rock climbs. They can certainly feel more serious. On Rhinog Fawr, the route is not laid down and marked in advance, and every man and woman up it is an explorer. The finding of a safe and feasible route is down to your own judgement, with potentially severe penalties for getting it wrong.

And this is the point of any adventurous activity, surely: that it makes you rely on yourself. Certainly in rock-climbing and scrambling you are ultimately responsible for your own safety. None of the routes in this book is unduly dangerous - if you approach it sensibly. If you don't, then all of the routes in this book are potentially dangerous - and so is everything else in life.

Enough of the sombre stuff. Scrambling and climbing are among the greatest pleasures in life, and Snowdonia is among the greatest places to enjoy them. Take care - but have fun!

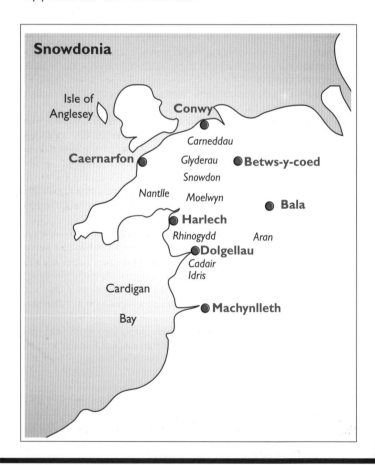

Ogwen Valley.

A single long valley gives access to the southern Carneddau, as well as to the following two sections, Tryfan and Glyderau. Strictly speaking the valley east of Llyn Ogwen is called Nant y Benglog and that to the west Nant Ffrancon, but climbers invariably refer to the whole as 'the Ogwen valley' or simply 'Ogwen'.

We could have filled this book with routes around this great valley. Nowhere in Snowdonia, indeed nowhere else in Britain, is there such a concentration of good scrambling and easy climbing. Ogwen has worked its magic on every generation of Welsh climbers. The earliest pioneers favoured the apparent security of the enclosed gullies, but well before the end of the 19th Century climbers were discovering the delights of the open slabs and ribs. The two Ordinary Routes, on Idwal Slabs (1897) and Milestone Buttress (1899), are fine examples. The area's popularity has continued to grow ever since, interrupted only by two world wars, and it saw the first great route of the post-war era with Chris Preston's ascent of Suicide Wall. Today that route's graded E2 5c, and even with sticky boots, chalk and micro-wires it is a test-piece of its grade. Of course it is way too hard for this book, but anyone descending from the Idwal Slabs will pass right below it.

Climbing in Ogwen is well into its second century and continues to attract vast numbers of devotees, most of them drawn by the easier routes. It's a racing certainty that more people have been introduced to 'real' climbing here than anywhere else.

As it is, this area does account for around half of the book, and accordingly we have subdivided it into three parts. Here we detail access to the Ogwen Valley, applicable to all three of the following sections Carneddau, Glyderau and Ogwen. The one exception is the northern approach to Craig yr Ysfa, full details of which are given at the start of the Carneddau section.

Access to Ogwen Valley

For the car user, with the main A5 running right through the valley, access could hardly be easier. The problem that can arise in busy periods is parking: spaces at Ogwen and in the lakeside lay-bys fill up remarkably quickly. The road is often lined with parked cars a long way to the east from the foot of Tryfan. It's not much fun changing your clothes at the roadside with juggernauts howling past at the maximum legal speed – and cars and motorbikes sometimes a good deal faster – only a couple of metres away.

Fortunately, there is an alternative, as the S3 Snowdon Sherpa bus service runs through the valley, connecting Bethesda and Ogwen with Pen y Pass, Capel Curig and Betws-y-Coed. Betws-y-Coed provides a link with the national rail network. The weakness of this service is the time of the last bus, which doesn't allow for long days on the crags. However there is a strong drive to improve the service – and the more people use it, the faster it is likely to develop.

Using the bus also opens up new possibilities, which offer a different shape to the day and new scenic perspectives. Take the bus, for instance, from Capel Curig to the shores of Llyn Ogwen and follow one of our expeditions onto Glyder Fach, but then, instead of descending back to Ogwen, follow the ridge eastward, most of it a gentle grassy descent, to Capel Curig. It's equally possible to descend to Pen y Pass or Pen-y-Gwryd.

Ogwen Valley Amenities

The Ogwen valley is quite sparsely populated; there are no pubs or hotels between Capel Curig and Bethesda and only a couple of B&Bs. There are, however, two campsites, both in the shadow of Tryfan (literally on some evenings). Gwern Gof Uchaf is very close to Tryfan Bach; Gwern Gof Isaf a little further up the valley. Both have fairly basic facilities and also bunkhouse accommodation. There is a Youth Hostel (Idwal Cottage) at Ogwen: a superb location but don't expect to turn up without booking and find a bed! The Climbers' Club Hut at Helyg has played a pivotal role in the history of climbing in the area: members of other clubs can use it, but it is very small and advance booking (hutbookings@climbers-club.co.uk) is essential. Those looking for hotel accommodation will need to head to Capel Curig or Betws-y-Coed.

Food and drink in the valley itself is only available from the tea-bar at Ogwen, where there are also public toilets. Apres-climb options include any of the three pubs in Capel Curig, where there are also several tea-rooms if you get there early enough. In the other direction, the Douglas Arms at Bethesda is a classic pub, with an old-fashioned atmosphere.

The Carneddau

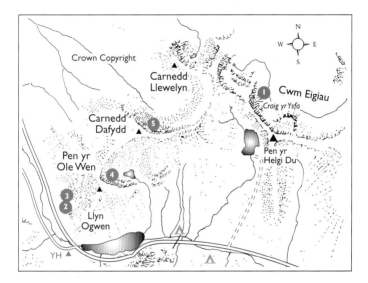

From the ever-popular Ogwen valley it's the blatantly rocky northern slopes of the Glyderau and, above all, the ragged outline of Tryfan that catch the eye. To the north of the valley, by contrast, the Carneddau appear as great rounded humps and ridges that promise great things to the walker but seem to have less to offer the dedicated crag-rat.

For the walker their promise is undoubtedly fulfilled, their long swelling ridges being among the best in Britain for striding out in solitude and space. But they have far more to offer the climber than first impressions suggest; for their lonely cwms hide some powerful crags. It's the Carneddau, not the Glyderau, that are home to the longest route in this book, the mighty Amphitheatre Buttress, which is a full day's work for all but a superhuman few. The scrambles on Llech Ddu and in Cwm Lloer are shorter and easier but share the brooding mountain atmosphere. In contrast, there are two short and sunny offerings on the Braich

Ty Du face, with easy access from the road – and a constant reminder of its proximity.

Northern Carneddau Access and Amenities

As well as the access from the Ogwen valley, already described, for Craig yr Ysfa access from the Conwy valley is an attractive alternative. For many people this will simply mean driving up the B5106 from Betws-y-Coed, but a night or two in the Conwy valley makes a refreshing change from the usual climbers' hot-spots. Trefriw makes a good base, with several pubs and restaurants, plus a fair selection of B & B accommodation and a couple of camping/caravan sites. The crag approach starts from Tal-y-Bont, which has a couple of pubs and the smarter Lodge Hotel.

Llyn Eigiau, seen on the northern approach to the Amphitheatre Buttress

Craig yr Ysfa Expedition

There could hardly be a better choice for the first route in the book: a long route on a remote crag, it has the expedition flavour in full measure. This is true mountaineering. There are no half-measures here, no easy way to change your mind part-way through. There's a long walk in, a long climb, and then a long walk out: simple, but not easy. It is unreservedly recommended, but only to those who already have a number of substantial V. Diff routes under their belts.

There's a persistent, though probably apocryphal, story that the crag was first discovered by telescope from Scafell in the Lake District. This would require quite exceptional atmospheric conditions, though is it definitely possible to make out the Lakeland peaks from Carnedd. But even on dimmer and more typical days, the outlook is expansive, stretching over deserted Cwm Eigiau and the rolling slopes of the Carneddau to the sea.

1. Amphitheatre Buttress 294m V. Diff
Guide time 5-6 hours

When ten-metre routes are described as 'classic', how do you describe Amphitheatre Buttress? 'Epic' would fit, except that in mountaineering parlance the word usually implies things going wrong. Amphitheatre Buttress is epic in the best sense: rich, complex and involving. It is the longest rock-climb in this book, and one of the longest climbs in England or Wales. Even by Scottish standards it is no small undertaking.

None of the climbing is desperately difficult, but routes of this length make extra demands on fitness, especially as you will almost certainly be climbing with a sack. Start early (this also helps to avoid queuing), pace yourself, eat and drink sensibly – and savour every magnificent minute!

There is a fair amount of vegetation on some sections but the route is well trodden and the harder climbing is on clean rock. Nevertheless the crag is high and north-facing and is best saved for a fine spell in summer or autumn.

First climbed in 1905.

Approaches: The usual approach is from the Ogwen Valley. However,

Craig yr Ysfa Expedition

the alternative northern approach, lonely and little-trodden, is more atmospheric and less strenuous.

Approach from the Ogwen Valley (1 1/2 hours)
The start is by the waterworks road to Ffynnon Llugwy reservoir. There is very limited parking by the gate and it is vital not to block access. Sherpa buses (service S3) pass this point.

The first stage is simply a boring slog up the dead straight road. For those with eyes in the backs of their heads, the expanding views relieve the monotony. The reservoir track levels out at last and then bends left. Leave it here for a small path on the right, passing a sheepfold. The path contours just above the lake for about 400m and then climbs, becoming progressively steeper. Good zigzags, which have benefited from restoration work, mean that the steep section is much pleasanter than it used to be. The path arrives at a narrow col (Bwlch Eryl Farchog).

Descend straight over the other side. The path zigzags down and then works leftward. When the path splits, take the right (lower) branch, still downhill, to pass a lone tree. About 20m below the tree a path breaks out left across the slope – now about two thirds of the way down the steepest ground – then zig-zags down an open grassy area. Cross a tongue of scree, then go round the foot of a rock rib and up slightly above a heathery shoulder. Follow the path along the base of the crag and then up again over scree, boulders and heather until the Amphitheatre opens out above. This is unmistakable, appearing as a huge gully, with its right wall culminating in a very impressive vertical face (climbed by the classic VS Mur y Niwl and a number of harder routes).

Northern approach (1 hour)
This is a pleasanter approach, though further from the main centres. It starts from Tal-y-Bont in the Conwy valley. A steep, narrow and twisting road ends at a parking area at SH731662. Follow the continuation track past the remains of the broken dam, forking right just before Hafod-y-rhiw, and forking right again to cross the little bridge above the lake head, then passing the white-shuttered Cwm Eigiau Cottage (714637). The track is good, and makes for easy progress right into the heart of the cwm. The crag looms over the upper cwm; go up the left side of the big tongue of scree which spills from the Amphitheatre.
Start at the foot of the apparently detached rib forming the left (south)

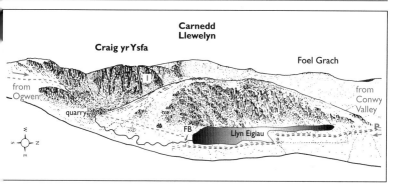

Carnedd Llewelyn

Craig yr Ysfa

Foel Grach

from Ogwen

from Conwy Valley

quarry

FB

Llyn Eigiau

P

W N S E

side of the Amphitheatre. Just to the right are some big boulders lying at a similar angle to the initial slabs.

1. (25m) It's possible to climb from the very foot, up a two-tier slab, but it's common to sneak on from the right about 10m up, scrambling up to a heathery ledge at the top of the slab's upper tier. A few moves up the slab above lead to a niche. Step out left from this onto another little slab, which proves quite delicate. Continue up a broken groove to reach a large ledge.

2. (30m) Carry on easily up the ridge for another 10m to another possible stance. Continue easily up another 7m to the foot of a short steep groove: make a move or two up this then pull out to the left. Belay just above on a ledge below a large leaning block.

3. (40m) Climb up immediately to the right of the block and then step out onto its top. Step across a gap onto the exposed slab above. Move up about 4m and then work left into a wide crack which provides a resting place. Step back right and climb the continuation of the slab, steep but seamed with deep cracks. Follow good but sometimes widely spaced holds, gradually trending back right to a spike on the right edge about 25m up the pitch.

It's possible to belay on the spike, but there's no real stance: consider it only if running low on gear or struggling with rope drag. Climb a short slabby groove above to a broad ledge and walk left along this to

Craig yr Ysfa Expedition

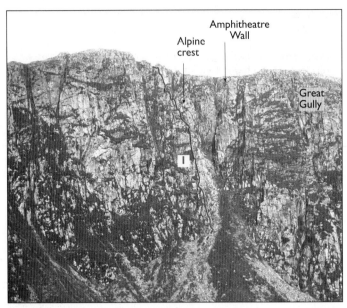

an obvious, easy groove. Climb this to a palatial stance below a steep 8m wall with several overhangs.

4. (12m) Reputedly the crux. Climb the right edge of the wall on polished holds to a block on the skyline. From the top of the block step round onto the Amphitheatre side. Use a thin crack, then holds on the arete, to reach a welcoming ledge.

5. (25m) 3m left of the point of arrival, climb a steep cracked wall for 10m. Swing out left to a small ledge, go up 2m and then step back right to a sloping ledge. Above this is an easy, broken but somewhat dirty groove, almost a path. Scramble up this for about 10m to a ledge with a prominent belay crack at the back.

6. (65m) Walking and easy scrambling on a well-trodden line. Various large spikes offer themselves if you feel the need to belay on this section. It ends

Craig yr Ysfa Expedition

abruptly at a bare rock platform beyond which the ridge continues as a sharp 'Alpine' crest. There's a useful block to belay on.

7. (35m) From the back right corner of the platform step down awkwardly into the gap beyond. Go up a little to a large gendarme, which is easily bypassed on the left. This is followed by a very awkward spiky knife edge. Take care to protect the second here: lots of long slings prove useful. Carry on along the crest until it runs out into a grassy slope.

8. (32m) There are two broken ridges above. Walk and scramble up towards the right-hand one. When you reach continuous rock at its base, climb up rightwards over blocks to a short horizontal knife-edge. There's a hanging slab just above. Long-legged climbers can make a big stride right to a spiky block below the right side of the slab: shorter people may need to step down and pull back up onto it. The crack near the slab's left edge welcomes fingers and nuts but there's a shortage of footholds. Go up the slab to a stance.

Edge of Amphitheatre Wall

altve start hidden

Craig yr Ysfa Expedition

Craig yr Ysfa Expedition

Bernie Carter on the Amphitheatre Buttress

9. (30m) Climb a steep blocky section to below the forbidding final wall. Climb a shallow chimney-groove near the wall's left side and make a hard pull onto the very edge about 20m above the stance. Swing round this edge onto the wall which overlooks the minor gully on the left. Discover, with relief, a diagonal line of flakes leading easily to the unaccustomed luxury of level ground.

Descent: Walk left (general heading a little east of south) following rough paths down the rocky ridge to Bwlch Eryl Farchog. The ridge is quite narrow and airy in places but there's nothing more than very simple scrambling. For those returning to Llyn Eigiau, descend leftward from the lowest point of the bwlch (as described for the later stages of the Ogwen approach to the crag). On reaching more open slopes below the crag, descend into the cwm to rejoin the outward route.

Next: for those returning to Ogwen, the obvious choice now would be to turn right and retrace the route of approach. However, there is much to be said for continuing straight ahead, along the narrow ridge and up the steep north-western flank of Pen yr Helgi Du. Overall it's not a lot more effort, is kinder on the feet and a lot more interesting. The re-ascent involves easy but entertaining scrambling (easy Grade 1).
As the ridge broadens out above the scrambling section, it is possible to contour rightwards and miss out the summit of Pen yr Helgi Du, but this saves only a few heartbeats of extra effort. From the summit head due south and pick up a good path down the long grassy spur of Y Braich. Follow this for two kilometres to a footbridge over a walled leat. Cross this and bear right, across a field to a stile in the bottom corner, close to some stone sheep pens. Cross the stile and continue down to a junction with a broad track. Turn right onto this and follow it down to the A5. The start of the waterworks road is about 300m to the right (west) along the road.

Pen yr Ole Wen Expedition

Pen yr Ole Wen extends south from the main bulk of the Carneddau and rises steeply from the shores of Llyn Ogwen. The zigzag path up the shaly south ridge of Pen yr Ole Wen, starting from the outflow of Llyn

Pen yr Ole Wen Expedition

Ogwen, is brutally steep and unremitting. Discerning walkers usually choose the gentler east ridge as a prelude to a traverse of the higher Carneddau tops. However, it is Pen yr Ole Wen's west flank that offers scrambling adventures overlooking the U-shaped valley of the Nant Ffrancon. The Braich Ty Du face is a maze of ridges, buttresses and rock walls separated by scree-filled gullies and heather slopes.

At first sight this huge complex face ought to provide lots of continuous scrambling and rock climbing. However, despite the great amount of rock hereabouts there are not many good routes to be found. A wide band of very steep heather and scree runnels at mid height means that to link the lower buttresses situated just above the A5 road with the ridges high up on the face, involves about 250m of very unpleasant ascent.

The popular Pinnacle Ridge route avoids the horrid heather at mid height altogether. It is accordingly a fairly short climb, with an easy approach. If you have only have a few hours to spare then Pinnacle Ridge, which is only about 25 minutes approach from Ogwen Cottage, offers an excellent outing. Despite being close to the road the climb is in a magnificent situation and has the feel of a big ridge. The castellated section at the top of the ridge also provides a short, but attractive and exposed, Grade 2 scramble as an alternative (Route 3 following).

2. Pinnacle Ridge 98m V. Diff
Guide time about 1 1/2 hours

First ascended in 1950, the ridge gives varied climbing, the highlight being the exposed traverse of the pinnacled crest on the final pitch. The crag is west facing, catching the afternoon sunshine and drying quickly after rain.

Approach: From Ogwen Cottage follow the A5 left (north-west) for 200m to cross the road bridge over Llyn Ogwen's outlet stream. Just across the bridge on the right, cross the Alf Embleton stile, turn left and follow a narrow path up the rocky staircase to the top of the first rise and three circular stone windbreaks. Continue up the south ridge of Pen yr Ole Wen on the steep main path for about 20m, then head left, traversing along a smaller, contouring path. This passes below several rock buttresses towards a longer and more continuous buttress which rises from just above the road and is topped by two prominent pinnacles forming the serrated skyline at the top of Pinnacle Ridge. The start of Pinnacle Ridge is high up on the far side of this continuous buttress. The faint path crosses a collapsed wall and then slants up across grass and scree towards a shoulder on the right side of the continuous buttress, just below those pinnacles.

The grassy gully to the right of the pinnacles is crossed by a stone wall, which abuts against the ridge just below the pinnacles. (The following Route 3 will start from just above this wall.) Traverse left below the wall and follow a faint footpath across a heather shoulder below the pinnacles. The path soon descends to a grassy slope a few metres below the actual start of Pinnacle Ridge.

Start at the foot of a clean slabby rib with 'PR' scratched on the rock. To the left of the rib is a bay of broken rock and heather.

1. (30m) Up the slabby rib. After a delicate start up small holds better ones soon appear and the slabby rib is followed to a large block at about 18m. Make an awkward high step into a groove to the right of the block, and follow this groove to easier ground to a ledge and large spike belays.

2. (22m) To the right of the belay is the foot of a square-cut groove. Ascend this groove for about 10m to a heather terrace. Scramble up easy-angled heather and rock to a sloping, heathery ledge with spike belay.

Pen yr Ole Wen Expedition

Pen yr Ole Wen Expedition

3. (23m) Traverse up and right over heather and rock to the point below a continuing ridgeline above. Good holds lead up to the ridge. Follow the ridge easily up to a ledge and spike belay.

4. (23m) Climb up to a small ledge below the first pinnacle. (The scramble Route 3 below enters from the right just below this point.) From the ledge climb a 3m wall using large flaky holds to gain a higher ledge at the base of the first pinnacle. The climb over the two sharp, slender pinnacles is very exciting and exposed; there are good sling runners over the pinnacles.

From the notch beyond the second pinnacle, climb a short rocky step to a heather shoulder and slender grassy col.

Descent: to regain the footpath at the stone wall below the pinnacles, ascend to the grassy col and traverse to the right into the broad, grassy gully which leads easily back down to the stone wall.

3. Pinnacle Ridge Scramble Grade 2
Vertical height 20m: guide time about 15 minutes

A pleasant outing, which takes advantage of the easier but exhilarating upper reaches of the previous route. Though short the route offers some very exposed scrambling on excellent rock. From the pinnacles you have a bird's-eye-view back across the Nant Ffrancon to Ogwen Cottage backed by Cwm Idwal and Glyder Fawr.

Approach as for the previous route to the shoulder below the pinnacles, then cross the wall at the base of the broad gully.

Start about 10m above the stone wall. Traverse left along an obvious grassy ramp to a rocky corner with the first of the pinnacles directly above. Climb the corner on good holds for about 3m to join the ridge. Scramble up Pinnacle Ridge for a few metres to a ledge just below the first pinnacle. From the ledge climb a steep 3m wall using large flaky holds to gain a higher ledge at the base of the first pinnacle.

Traverse across the right-hand (Ogwen) side of the pinnacles on large holds in a very exposed position. Make an awkward step across to a notch beyond the second pinnacle, and climb a short rocky step to a heather shoulder and slender grassy col.

Descent: is as described for Route 2, above.

Pen yr Ole Wen Expedition

And Now?
Continuations over the Carneddau ridges are at the end of the following Route 4.

Craig Lloer Expedition

On the eastern flank of Pen yr Ole Wen lies the ice-carved rocky Cwm Lloer containing the lake of Fynnon Lloer (Spring of the Moon). The most prominent crag in the cwm is Craig Lloer, whose left edge provides a superbly exposed scramble – the Craig Lloer Spur. The cliff is delightfully secluded and is a great place for scramblers who want to avoid the polished rock and associated crowds of the more popular Ogwen routes. Craig Lloer faces north-east and catches the morning sunshine; it dries quickly and the rock is excellent. Above the cliff a broad ridge leads pleasantly up to the summit of Pen yr Ole Wen.

4. Craig Lloer Spur Grade 3
Vertical height about 75m; guide time about 1 hour.

Approach: Start from the bridge at Glan Dena (Grid ref: SH668605) alongside the A5 where there are numerous car parking places. Sherpa (S3) buses pass here.

Follow the track to Tal y Llyn Ogwen farm and just before reaching the buildings turn up right alongside a wall to a stile. Go over the stile and follow a waymarked grassy path, boggy in places, up the steep hillside mainly west of the Afon Lloer, to a stone wall. Beyond the wall the path enters the cwm where the path forks, the left branch aiming for the foot of the rocky East Ridge, a popular way up Pen yr Ole Wen; the right branch continues along to the lake.

The most prominent crag in the cwm is Craig Lloer, situated above screes on the southern slopes on the far side of Ffynnon Lloer. It forms the nose at the bottom of a long, broken spur rising to the summit of Pen yr Ole Wen.

The Craig Lloer buttress at the foot of the spur is triangular-shaped. It consists of a series of steep ribs, these being separated by grassy grooves that taper towards the top. The left boundary of the buttress is defined by a steep gully with a scree fan at its foot: to the left of the gully

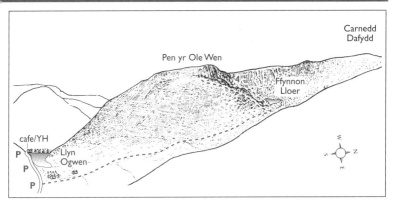

are three bands of steep vegetated rocks.

A direct way up the left edge of the Craig Lloer buttress, overlooking the steep gully, is the Eastern Arete climb (50m, Diff). Two thirds of the way up the buttress, this climb ascends directly up a prominent slab of pale rock. Our scramble follows a similar line but avoids the main difficulties by climbing up the right side of the pale slab. Above the main buttress, it will follow the Craig Lloer Spur to the summit of Pen yr Ole Wen.

Follow the lake's left-hand shore along a small path. Fork up left on an even smaller path that slants across the screes that emerge from the steep gully.

Start at the bottom left corner of the main Craig Lloer Buttress, right beside the steep gully mentioned above. The left edge of the buttress, overlooking the gully, is formed by a steep ridge, with some tilted blocks at its foot.

Avoid the tilted blocks by ascending a smooth slab to their right for about 6m to gain the ridge. Alternatively an easier start can be taken to the left of the blocks to reach the same point. Continue easily up the ridge over small blocks for about 10m to a larger one straddling the ridge. This block is split by a narrow 3m high crack, which can be climbed directly by a positive approach involving a high step up the crack to reach large holds. An easier alternative is a wide crack round to the left, regaining the ridge above the cracked block.

Craig Lloer Expedition

to Pen yr Ole-wen

Continue easily up the ridge for about 12m to a broken heathery ledge and block at the foot of a steep smooth slab. This is the pale slab already mentioned above, whose direct ascent is part of the Eastern Arete rock climb. Our route will avoid this difficulty by traversing out right in a very exposed position where a slip would have serious consequences. Some may appreciate a rope on this short section.

From the block at the foot of the pale slab, traverse right along heather ledges for about 6m to their end. The traverse can be protected by a sling over a large spike about 2m above the ledges. Continue the traverse right for a further 3m using good handholds on top of a flake. Aim for the obvious notch on the skyline.

The situation here is very exposed with a steep drop down a groove to your right. Thankfully a couple of moves above the notch lead quickly onto a ledge and block belay above all difficulties.

Craig Lloer Expedition

Continue up short walls and heather ledges, which lead easily to some very knobbly rock and then a gap. Cross the gap and scramble over more blocks and up a short chimney to easier ground and the neck of the buttress abutting against the hillside about 75m above the start.

Descent: if you want to return to the foot of the buttress, then walk a few steps left to go down the steep gully already mentioned on the left boundary of the buttress. This is steep and awkward in places.

And now? Having gained all that height it would be a pity to miss out the summit of Pen yr Ole Wen. Ascend the stony slope up the broad upper spur to reach a band of vegetated broken rock, which is breached by an easy gully. Continue up the ridge to join the East Ridge path near the summit.

From the summit of Pen yr Ole Wen you can descend its East Ridge to the outflow from Ffynnon Lloer and follow the path back down to the farm at Tal y Llyn Ogwen. The descent of the east ridge is far less stressful on your knees than the very steep southern ridge of Pen yr Ole Wen. If you started from Ogwen Cottage you could now return along the pleasant path on the north shore of Llyn Ogwen.

Alternatively you could continue from the summit of Pen yr Ole Wen around the rim of Cwm Lloer up to Carnedd Dafydd and along to Carnedd Llewelyn, returning into the Ogwen Valley via Ffynnon Llugwy Reservoir. Or if you started from Capel Curig by bus, you could return down the quite rough south ridge of Pen Llithrig y Wrach, swinging left at the ridge foot to a leat bridge (Grid ref: SH716609). A grass path then leads to Tal-y-waun and the A5 near Capel Curig.

Cwm Llafar Expedition

Hemmed in by the two highest peaks in the Carneddau and big enough to remind one of a broad Highland glen, Cwm Llafar is as breathtakingly beautiful as any valley in Snowdonia. Its headwall appears impenetrable; a broken bastion of black rock that casts long shadows over the remote, boulder-strewn slopes below. Yet there is a way through; a devious line that traces a narrow rocky spine almost to the summit of Carnedd Dafydd itself. Known as Crib Lem or the Llech Ddu Spur, this

Craig Lloer Expedition

is the finest scramble of its grade in the Carneddau.

5. Llech Ddu Spur Grade 1

Vertical height about 200m: guide time about 1 hour (from the grassy plat-form to the bottom of the scree-covered summit dome).

A straightforward and fairly easy scramble along a broad rocky ridge, punctuated with huge blocks, flakes and pinnacles. The rock is sound throughout, even in the wet, and there are plenty of different lines if any section looks a little too daunting. The positions are fantastic all the way along, with plenty of exposure and huge views over the head of Cwm Llafar to Carnedd Llewelyn and Yr Elen.

Approach from Gerlan, on the eastern edge of Bethesda. Gerlan is most easily reached from the A5, just south of Bethesda, by turning up Braichmelyn, climbing up through the village, and then turning right at a crossroads. Early starters will find roadside parking (grid ref SH 633662) as the houses gradually subside. If this is full, there's more space back towards the village centre. Sherpa buses (service S3) link Bethesda, Ogwen, Capel Curig and Pen y Pass.

Walk up the lane, Gerlan Road, south-east out of the village, and bear right at a fork to cross a bridge over the Afon Llafar. Climb up to the end of the road and bear left, up a drive and past a waterworks sign. At the next gate (marked 'Private') bear right over a stile, and then turn left to follow the field edge up to another stile. Cross this and turn right, following marker posts past some ruined buildings and out onto open ground with the river down to your left.

Now continue up the valley, with the Afon Llafar always on your left, for approximately 3km until the way ahead levels and you are faced with the imposing cliffs of Llech Ddu to the right.

To the right of the cliffs, you'll see a steep, scree-covered bank that leads up into a secluded hanging valley called Cwmglas Bach. The scrambling is going to start on the left wall of this cwm.

Turn right, away from the main path, and cross some boggy level ground, past some large boulders, to a zigzagging path that leads up the left-hand end of the scree bank. For most of the year there will be a small waterfall to your right. Continue up until you are deep within Cwmglas Bach. As you near the steep back wall, roughly level with the

Cwm Llafar Expedition

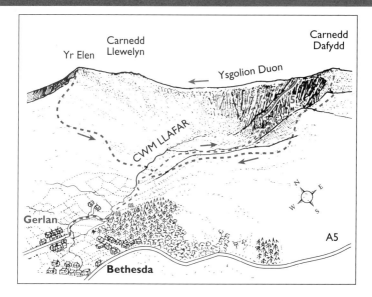

In the illustration: Yr Elen, Carnedd Llewelyn, Carnedd Dafydd, Ysgolion Duon, CWM LLAFAR, Gerlan, Bethesda, A5

foot of Craig y Cwmglas Bach – the spire-topped crag to your right – you will make out a rough path turning back sharp left. This follows an easy-angled ramp of bilberry and heather up between rock bands towards the top of the Llech Ddu crags. You'll pass through a band of quartz and end up on a broad grassy platform on the crest of the ridge.

Start from the grassy platform on the crest of the ridge, with the Llech Ddu crag, which you can no longer see, directly below you.

Climb the rocky wall directly above you; either directly or by one of the many paths that avoid the steepest rock. Continue upwards over a couple of small rock steps, until you pass a sizeable pinnacle down to your right.

The ridge narrows now and although it's never really knife-edge, there are plenty of flakes and pinnacles to scramble over if you so wish. There's a path that crosses back and forth around most of the obstacles if you'd rather take the easy route.

After a few minutes, you'll scramble up onto a slabby sloping table that's a little awkward to descend from – this is the crux of the route

Cwm Llafar Expedition

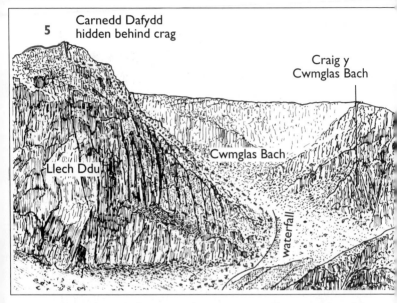

Carnedd Dafydd
hidden behind crag

5

Craig y
Cwmglas Bach

Cwmglas Bach

Llech Ddu

waterfall

but again, it's avoidable to the left if you'd rather. The remainder of the ridge consists of a series of rock bands broken by grassy sections. Make them as hard or as easy as you like and when they finally peter out, keep ahead to cross scree slopes to the summit.

Descent: Scramblers can choose to descend directly; heading north to rejoin the edge of the escarpment overlooking Cwm Llafar, and then following this down, over Mynydd Ddu, to rejoin the Cwm Llafar path at the bottom.

And Now? Those looking for a truly memorable day should continue from Carnedd Dafydd's summit east then north-east to Carnedd Llewelyn and then break off north-west to ascend Yr Elen by a pleasant and mildly rocky ridge. To descend, keep ahead (north-west) from the summit of Yr Elen, until you've cleared the rocky outcrops of Foel Ganol, and then bear left to cross wet ground to the Afon Llafar. Ford the stream and rejoin the path you followed earlier in the day.

Cwm Llafar Exp

Steph Duits on the Llech Du Spur

Cwm Llafar Expedition

Scrambling up the North Ridge of Tryfan

Tryfan

Tryfan is unique: the only peak in Wales that can't be ascended on unassisted feet. With careful route selection and a very good sense of balance, it is possible to disprove this claim all the way to the summit ridge. But, without using hands, only a champion gymnast will manage to top out on the twin monoliths of Adam and Eve which crown the peak.

And though avoiding the use of hands may be fun for a while, it ultimately misses out on the tactile pleasure of so much good rock. From most angles, and especially when approaching from the east Tryfan appears to be all rock.

In basic form Tryfan is a simple north-south ridge. The East Face, with its neatly aligned gullies and buttresses, has the grandest climbing routes. Initially it may appear daunting, but a second look reveals that the overall angle is moderate. And hands-on acquaintance demonstrates that there's an abundance of excellent holds.

The West Face is more chaotic. It offers prospects to the scrambler/climber with a hunger for exploration, but a large dose of patience is also likely to be needed. Promising lines peter out into thigh-deep heather or, just as frequently, stutter to a halt beneath a short smooth barrier. The dip of the strata, which creates so many incut holds on the East Face, has the opposite effect on the west.

Low down, before

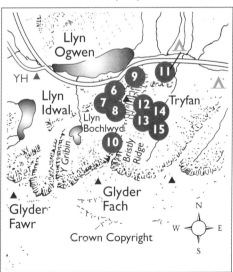

the North Ridge and West Face really take on separate identities, is Milestone Buttress. Its closeness to the road is either a blessing or a curse. It certainly isn't the place for a wilderness experience. Rather than contemplating the beauties of nature, you may find yourself reflecting on how a 750cc Ducati can make more noise than a 17-litre Volvo artic. The valley is also much used by the RAF, though not at weekends. Watching Tornados scream down the valley – at eye level from Milestone Buttress – is a distinctively Ogwen experience. You wonder how they can make the hard right turn at Idwal Falls, but they always have done (so far).

For Location map, access and food facts, see 'Ogwen Valley Intro' at the start of the book.

Milestone Buttress Crag Day
192m climbing, up to V. Diff

Since it lies at the foot of Tryfan, this can easily be turned into the first stage of an expedition, whether by scrambling up the easy North Ridge, working round to the East Face climbs, or exploring the little-frequented West Face. However, as a self-contained cragging day it is by no means to be despised. There is a lot of good climbing here, on friendly grey rock which is absolutely clean, sometimes a little too clean. Short pitches, generous stances, and the regular occurrence of huge holds all conspire to give the routes an old-fashioned air, despite the constant, noisy presence of the 21st Century. But it's not all dead easy: there are frequent reminders that the old-timers were actually very capable climbers. Don't underestimate Milestone Buttress.

6. Ordinary Route 101m Diff
Guide time about 2 hours

'Ordinary Route' sounds a bit disparaging. (It may be worth recalling that one of the three routes of this name in North Wales is an E5!) None of it is desperate, but the climbing is absorbing, requiring a variety of techniques, and several pitches have a strong individual character. The descent is sufficiently involved and exposed that it's worth staying roped for most of it; it is described as such and included in the overall

Milestone Buttress Crag Day

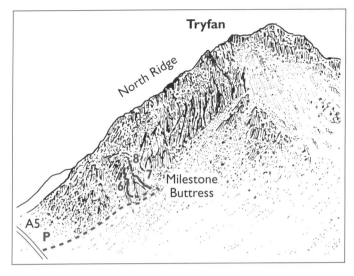

length and timing for the route
    First climbed in 1899.

Approach: The crag stands prominently above a bend in the A5 near the head of Llyn Ogwen. There are several lay-bys in the vicinity and Sherpa buses (service S3) run along the road. The eponymous milestone can still be seen in the nearest lay-by. From a turnstile near the east end of this lay-by (SH663603) follow a pitched path with huge steps: this also leads to the North Ridge of Tryfan. Ignore the first stile on the right and carry on to a second. Cross this and make a descending traverse to pass below the scrappy bottom tier of crag. There are climbs on this, but they are rarely bothered with. Follow the rough path up right and back left to a slanting terrace below the skinned rock of the crag proper.

Start: just a few metres from the left end of the terrace, below the steep termination of the central ridge.

1. (30m) Climb some big rock steps that lead round to the left of the central ridge; then step left into a groove. Ascend this to a steepening at

Milestone Buttress Crag Day

a block; climb awkwardly straight over the block or, more easily, go round its left side and back right onto its top.

A few metres higher, the main groove-line deteriorates into heathery steps. Here it's better, though harder, to follow a shallow groove incised

into the left flank of the central ridge. Either way leads to a big ledge on the domed crest of the ridge, with a sharp projecting spike just above.

2. (14m) Climb up behind the spike, then traverse left a couple of metres and climb a short corner crack to a good ledge. On the right is a large flake. Step from this into the thigh-width crack above and do the hokey-cokey. Long arms definitely help here. The final jugs are most welcoming but getting to them can be a real struggle. Just above is a sheltered ledge.

3. (14m) On the left is a 'needle's eye' in the rock. Climb onto the edge directly above it. It looks as if there's nothing but a void beyond, but the decisive step reveals a straightforward foot-ledge running back towards Tryfan. Follow it for 4m to the foot of a wide deep chimney. This can be climbed elegantly using holds on the outside, but it is more satisfying as well as more secure to climb just inside by some vigorous squirming. At the top choose from a variety of perches on wedged boulders.

4. (8m) Climb the triangular slab above: ideally straight up the middle, more easily up the right edge, more easily still by sloping off into the gully on its right. By whichever route, arrive in an enclosed bay, overlooked by the steep tower of the Central Block on the left. Belay at the back of the bay, towards the right-hand side.

5. (7m) Climb the open chimney at the back of the bay, with blessed simplicity, past several spikes to an open grassy bay. This is the traditional end of the route.

6. (20m) Climb a short corner at back right of the bay, then make a long traverse right over easy but exposed slabs to a notch in the arete. Many leaders may feel little need of protection on the traverse, but should consider the second's feelings too. Belay at the notch, which looks down into a steep gully beyond.

7. (12m) From the notch, step down 3m to a ledge running out on the opposite wall of the gully, then traverse right again until a final step down gains broad rock ledges. It is now safe to unrope as the rest of the gully descent is simple, obvious and eroded.

Milestone Buttress Crag Day

Next: The descent gully leads down alongside the western edge of the crag. The three huge stacked blocks that form The Pulpit are blatantly obvious from this angle. A clean rib runs up to ledges just below them.

Bernie Carter on Pitch 2 of the Pulpit Route, Milestone Buttress

Milestone Buttress Crag Day

7. Pulpit Route 50m Moderate
Guide time about 40 minutes to junction with Ordinary Route

Hundreds, probably thousands, have taken their first steps on rock on this route, and there could hardly be a better introduction; just hard enough to be interesting, but without a single nasty bit to spoil the pleasure. The obvious continuation by Ivy Chimney, though no less worthwhile, is a different kettle of fish, and they are best considered as two separate routes. The top of Pulpit Route joins the traverse and descent already described for Ordinary Route.

First climbed in 1911.

Approach: If coming to Pulpit Route direct from the A5 below, branch right when you reach the terrace below the crag, and follow the base of the crag up and right until it swings round into a big open gully, which marks the right-hand end of the good rock.

Start: At the foot of a clean rib, which runs up just right of two rowan trees in a crack. An overhanging block, the base of the Pulpit, looms above.

1. (29m) Climb the rib and the slab above, all delightfully simple, to a ledge just below the overhanging base of the Pulpit. Climb the slab on its right, with one awkward move, to belay on the Pulpit.

2. (21m) A peach of a pitch. From the highest block step onto the slab on the left. Climb up and over a slight overlap just right of a holly – if the right sequence of holds is found this is much easier than it looks. Go up a couple of metres and move diagonally left to behind a flake (possible stance, 10m so far).

Just above is a steep barrier with one obvious rectangular cut-out. Step onto a tiny hanging slab just below this, where some providential holds come into reach. Move up through the cut-out, and continue straight up for 8m to a ledge and large belays.

Next: From here the rightward traverse on Pitch 6 of Ordinary Route is a few metres higher, giving an easy escape. But if you're up for a fight and had extra porridge this morning, Ivy Chimney should not be missed. It's the obvious dark cleft near the right end of the steeper rock above.

Just right of the chimney is a pointed pillar, while to its left is a corner where birch and rowan grow.

8. Ivy Chimney 41m V. Diff
Guide time: 45 minutes

A grand chimney of the gloriously old-fashioned kind, with an explosive finish in a position that seems thoroughly modern.

Start at the top of Pulpit Route (or midway along the traverse of Pitch 6, Ordinary Route)

1. (18m) As on Pitch 6 of Ordinary Route, traverse right, across easy but exposed slabs, to a notch in their bounding edge. Step up from here and traverse right, round the head of a small branch gully, then step up awkwardly onto a slabby shelf which leads to the base of the chimney.

2. (16m) A steep move on jugs gets you into the chimney, and delivers an immediate sense of commitment. The depths beckon but if you don't go too far in a helpful subsidiary slab on the left can be used, until it is possible – if not essential – to launch oneself into daylight through a slit on the right. This brings abrupt exposure, and wonderful jugs just out of reach. Once these are grasped, they allow a final wild move to a stance in a trough with great views of the rest of the party.

3. (7m) The steep wall directly above the stance can be climbed by its exposed right edge, or by a deep jamming crack up its centre, or a combination; but if the nerves are shot there's an easier alternative on the left in the form of a tapering slab and short V-groove. All ways lead to a good belay just above.

Descent: Go up a few metres until above some piled blocks then round right to the head of a steep gully. In descent this is good Grade 2 scrambling. At the bottom there's an awkward step down from a smooth shelf. There is usually a pile of blocks below to make the step a bit shorter.

   The route here joins Ordinary Route at the broad rock ledges near the end of its Pitch 7. The rest of the descent is simple, obvious and eroded.

Milestone Buttress Crag Day

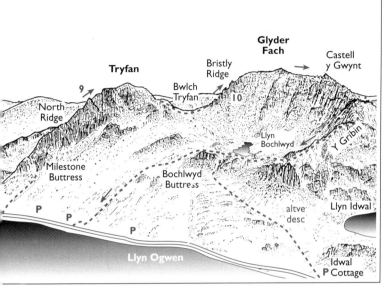

Tryfan & Bristly Ridge Expedition
800m scrambling: up to Grade 1

One of the classic UK mountain days; Tryfan's North Ridge and Glyder Fach's Bristly Ridge combine to produce an outstanding outing of grade-one scrambling that has few equals. This is scrambling heaven; exposed and serious enough to offer the five-star, big-mountain experience, yet technically easy enough for any fit walker, with a head for heights, to scale comfortably. If that isn't enough, the hands-on action starts just minutes away from the roadside and finally peters out just a few paces from the summit of Wales' sixth highest peak. True rock-addicts can even continue over Castell y Gwynt and keep their hands in meaningful employment for the descent of Gribin Ridge. It's little wonder that so many folk take the first awkward steps of their scrambling career on these bold and rocky prows.

Tryfan & Bristly Ridge

Tryfan

North
Ridge

Bristly
Ridge

Glyder
Fach
→

10

Bwlch
Tryfan

9

Milestone
Buttress

P

Tryfan & Bristly Rideg Expedition

9. Tryfan North Ridge Grade 1

Vertical Height 550m: guide time 2 hours from the first scrambling moves to the summit.

From the first bold move, just a few metres above the busy A5, to the last energetic pull-up beneath the imposing blocks of Adam and Eve, this is a straightforward and relatively easy scramble, although you can make it considerably more difficult if you want to. There is an almost infinite choice of lines, although most of them do tend to funnel into certain sections that have been elaborated on in the route description. Most (but not all) of the trickier sections can be bypassed using steep grassy paths. There is little need to worry about route finding, as long as you stick close to the crest of the ridge and avoid scrambling up anything that you couldn't safely climb back down again. Usually there will be a choice of plainly-trodden lines. The rock is superb throughout and provides plenty of grip, even on the wettest of days.

Approach from the A5. Sherpa buses (service S3) run along here. Leave the road at a kissing gate, marked with a footpath sign, at the foot of the prominent prow of Tryfan's North Ridge. This is approximately 300m west of the eastern tip of Llyn Ogwen.

Make your way up the man-made path, with a wall on your right, and ignore two stiles (these lead to Milestone Buttress), until your way ahead is blocked by a steep crag. Bear left and follow the path upwards, along the foot of the ridge. Continue for a couple of minutes until you are nearly on the apex of the shoulder that leads from the crest of the ridge down to the A5. **Start** here.

Choose one of any number of small polished niches that break up the wall at the foot of the ridge. Now continue directly upwards. Steep steps of polished rock, linked by well-worn tracks, point the way in the early stages. There are plenty to choose from so simply aim to stick as close to the crest of the ridge as possible and everything will come back together as you gain height and the ridge narrows.

At about half height, you'll reach a broad ledge, instantly recognisable by the Cannon Stone: a recumbent pinnacle, propped on a large quartz block and pointing out across the valley like a cannon guarding the mountain. Next up comes a small plateau, marked with a cairn, and after this, another balanced pinnacle reaffirms your position. Pass this pinnacle to its left, and scramble up a short wall before continuing to a short down-climb, which is best tackled to the left (facing out).

The next plateau, recognised by a very steep face directly ahead, marks a major milestone, as all the various lines are funnelled through this point. The steep wall ahead can be climbed directly at Grade 2; it's steep and exposed on large, well-used holds.

But to stay at comfy Grade 1, turn right, to contour around the face, and you'll come to the foot of a steep and strenuous boulder-filled gully.

Tryfan & Bristly Ridge Expedition

Climb this − definitely the crux of the route but still not particularly difficult − and at the top, you'll stand on the North Peak, with a shallow saddle separating you from the main summit. Drop into the saddle and climb easily up to Adam and Eve.

Next: From here, the route will drop into the deep col ahead, Bwlch Tryfan, before climbing the blunt comb of Bristly Ridge to the summit of Glyder Fach. First up is Tryfan's South Peak. Scramble down into the shallow col that separates the two summits and then clamber up onto South Peak's slabby top. The lower rocky protrusion directly ahead now is the Far South Peak. This could be avoided by a good track on the right; but, for purity of line, keep to the crest and scale this final jagged outpost of Tryfan, especially as it offers a good opportunity to recce the way ahead. From here, drop slightly to the right to make an easy bouldery scramble down and then contour around left into Bwlch Tryfan.

10. Bristly Ridge Grade 1
Vertical height around 250m: guide time about 1 hour from the low point of Bwlch Tryfan

This makes a natural continuation of the North Ridge and, in quality, offers more of the same thing, although sadly, not as long. The highlights are the giant pinnacles that punctuate the otherwise blunt arete. These provide a few awkward moments but as the whole ridge can be flanked on either side, there's not really anything to worry about. The last few metres give the whole outing a real mountaineering perspective, with the ridge finally relenting just a short stroll from the jumbled boulders of Glyder Fach's 994m summit.

Approach: Drop into Bwlch Tryfan, keeping the wall on your left, and as it starts to climb again, turn away from it, half-right, to contour beneath the foot of the first craggy outcrop. Once past this, head directly up again towards a pronounced gully dividing the wide lower portion of Bristly Ridge.

Start at the foot of the gully, which is well-trodden and partly blocked by a jammed boulder 20m above.

The way ahead is easiest if you stick to the line of the gully but the

Tryfan & Bristly Rideg Expedition

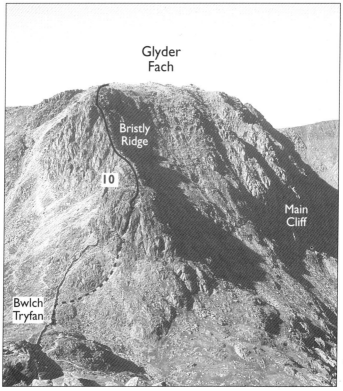

Glyder
Fach

Bristly
Ridge

10

Main
Cliff

Bwlch
Tryfan

Tryfan & Bristly Ridge Expedition

sport is much better if you scale the wall to the right of it.

Either way, head upwards for a few metres and cross a path that runs across the top of this first steep section. Now continue up the gully on good holds, to a very steep headwall that is best tackled on the left. This leads onto the crest of the ridge.

From here, try to keep as close to the crest as possible, with exciting drops to the left. The ridge narrows and rises to a rocky turret that should be crossed and then descended to the left. This leads into a deep gap in the ridge and ahead now is an intimidating pinnacle, the Great Pinnacle.

Tryfan & Bristly Rideg Expedition

Go right, through the gap, and then slant up to the left, around the base of this pinnacle, into a groove on its left. This is gently-angled with good holds, and leads back onto the crest. Sadly, shortly after this section, the angle relents and the scrambling is over. The ridge dips slightly and then delivers you easily onto the boulder-strewn summit plateau of Glyder Fach. The famous Cantilever rock is just a few paces to the left.

And now?

A quick visit to the summit of Glyder Fach will be followed with a direct descent of the rough and scrambly ridge of Y Gribin back into Cwm Bochlwyd.

Follow the main path that leads easily right (south-west), past some rocky spikes, towards the huge pile of boulders that make up Glyder Fach's summit. From here, follow the escarpment edge west until you reach the spectacular pinnacled turrets of Castell y Gwynt. And then, keeping this to your right, drop steeply down over jumbled boulders before bearing around to the right into a long col (Bwlch y Ddwy-Glyder). Alternatively, Castell y Gwynt can be scrambled over at around Grade 1.

The way ahead splits in the Bwlch y Ddwy-Glyder, with the left hand, lower, path heading up directly towards the summit of Glyder Fawr; but instead take the right hand, upper path running along the escarpment edge to a cairned prow that marks the top of Y Gribin.

From the cairn, bear right (north) to follow the ridge down. Keep to the crest for some easy scrambling or drop further to the left to follow a steep and, in places, loose path with few difficulties.

At 750m, the ridge levels to a grassy plateau that offers easy walking and good views. Continue ahead to the toe of the ridge and descend some pitched path to a broken wall. Here a path right leads down to the outflow of Llyn Bochlwyd.

Bus travellers can turn left here and drop down alongside the cascades to follow the obvious path to Ogwen Cottage. Those returning to a car parked near the start should cross the outflow stream and continue around the lake shore for 100m, before bearing left (north-east), to follow a clear path, which contours the hillside before descending to the road.

Left: Steph Duits scrambling on Bristly Ridge

Tryfan & Bristly Ridge Expedition

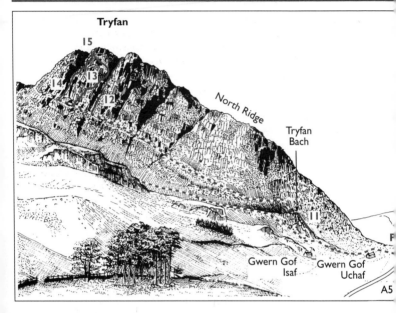

Tryfan

15

14 13

12

North Ridge

Tryfan Bach

11

Gwern Gof Isaf

Gwern Gof Uchaf

F

A5

Tryfan East Face Expedition
395m climbing, up to V.Diff; 200m Grade 1 scrambling (descent)

The routes on Tryfan's East Face have maintained their popularity for succeeding generations of climbers, loftily ignoring mere fads and fashions. It's not hard to see why, as they offer a recipe that comes close to perfection: routes of good length (but not too long), on rock that is mostly sound and mostly clean, in a true mountain situation and leading to a summit, or at least to the high cock's-comb crest of the mountain. And, with an early start, you can do most or all of the climb in the sun as well.

For many people, to do one of these routes, continue to the summit and then descend either via Cwm Tryfan or Cwm Bochlwyd, makes for a wonderful mountain day; satisfying without being exhausting. But unlike Lliwedd or Craig yr Isfa, you don't have to be superhuman to do two of the routes in the same day, and the descent of Central Buttress

Tryfan East Face

makes for a straightforward but interesting connection.

However, the most complete mountaineering approach is to do a route on one of the lower crags first: either Milestone Buttress or Tryfan Bach. The link-up from Milestone is intricate and time-consuming; Tryfan Bach is therefore recommended, with the added advantage that the ultimate objective is always in sight.

11. Tryfan Bach (left edge and ridge) 41m Diff plus scrambling
Guide time about 1 hour

Tryfan Bach, or Little Tryfan, is one of the classic beginner's crags, populated by bewildered teenagers in squashy trainers and outsize helmets. It may seem a bit of a circus, but this should not obscure the fact that it is a shapely crag of excellent rock. The apparently smooth slab is seamed with cracks and well-provided with holds; a determined search for the

Tryfan
Bach

Tryfan East Face Expedition

blankest bits may just yield short stretches of Severe climbing. The left edge is recommended because it is a little less busy, but all the obvious lines go at no more than Diff standard. Once on the crest above the main slab, the crowds are left behind, but a step in this upper ridge actually provides the most challenging moment of the route.

Approach: The crag is most easily reached from the farm at Gwern Gof Uchaf. Sherpa buses (Service S3) pass the entrance. Pass left of the farmhouse to a stile and then bear right on a well-worn path towards the crag, seen here from behind as a rather broken rocky ridge. In about 5 minutes the path passes under the nose of the crag and the main slab swings into view.

The crag is also easily approached from any of the parking spaces below the north ridge of Tryfan. From a gate and stile (SH668605) near the west end of a straight stretch of the A5, an obvious fenced track leads to Gwern Gof Uchaf, while a narrow path leads more directly to the crag.

Start at the bottom left corner of the big sheet of slab.

1. (16m) Climb the slab, keeping as close to the left edge as possible, then step round left around the slab's edge onto a comfortable ledge set into the steep wall on the left.

2. (12m) Step back onto the slab and continue up in much the same vein to large grassy ledges at the top of the slab.

Scramble rightwards over broken outcrops close to the ridge crest for about 25m until a steep wall blocks the way.

3. (13m) At the foot of the wall, just to right of its highest part, are some large blocks. Climb over these to gain a steep groove. Climb this with interest and pull out onto easier ground.

The ridge crest continues at a much easier angle. Scramble at will, over or round the various outcrops, until the ridge levels out.

Next: *from Tryfan Bach to Heather Terrace and Tryfan's East Face*
Follow the ridge of Tryfan Bach until a stone wall is met. (If crowds force you to miss out the climb on Tryfan Bach, walk up under its west face

Tryfan East Face Expedition

to reach the wall). Follow this rightward, without crossing it, across a vague, almost level saddle. Another path joins from the right – this one comes from the foot of the North Ridge – and the two converge into a short gully. Its right wall is very steep rock.

At the top of the gully – level with the top of the rock wall – there's a broad terrace on the right which would take you onto to the North Ridge. For the East Face, however, go almost horizontally left on a narrow but clear path. This soon begins to climb again, quite steadily, with odd steps of easy scrambling. You are now on Heather Terrace, though its 'terrace' status is less clear than it seems from afar. The upper slopes of Tryfan rise on your right, initially as a chaos of rock and heather. The first real landmark is a 25m buttress with some sizeable overhangs near its foot: Bastow Buttress. The path passes immediately below this to cross the foot of a distinct gully, quite open but still well-defined. This is Bastow Gully.

The path climbs up more steeply, over or round some large boulders, then crosses below a slightly deeper gully (Nor' Nor' Gully). Now above the path there's another area of rock, steep and partly overhanging low down, followed by an indistinct gully (Green Gully). Just a few metres after crossing this, look for a polished groove with 'GA' scratched on the rock and, as often as not, a queue of climbers below it. This is the start of Grooved Arete. This is probably the best-known climb on Tryfan but, as it's bordering on Severe, just a little too hard for this book.

The path continues climbing for another 50 metres then almost levels out. Stop here, just before the opening of North Gully.

12. North Buttress 185m Diff
Guide time about 2 1/2 hours

Of the major Tryfan routes, this is the one that was left out of the influential book Classic Rock, and as a result seems relatively neglected (but only relatively). Traffic on the lower reaches is added to by climbers heading for the excellent middle-grade routes on Terrace Wall and Belle Vue Bastion.

It is a route of three distinct sections. Entertaining and surprisingly strenuous climbing for the first three pitches is followed by a more broken section; this is best dispatched quickly by the easiest line, little more than walking, to get to the true delights above. A flank attack on Terrace

Wall is followed by an intricate and exposed traverse across its upper reaches to the promised land of Belle Vue Terrace. One feels privileged to be here.

First climbed in 1899.

Start: the wall to the right of North Gully has a pronounced rib and groove structure. The second groove across from the gully, about 10m in, has NB scratched at its base.

1. (24m) Climb the groove, fairly strenuously, for 16m to a possible stance. Go straight up over blocks then step left onto a sharp little rib below an overhang; from the top of the rib pull rightwards through the overhang. There are good jugs but not quite enough for the feet. Climb the short groove above, pulling out right to a level, roomy stance.

2. (19m) Behind the stance is a large groove, with a steep projecting rib to its left. The rib can be climbed in its entirety but is delicate and not easy to protect: good V.Diff. Instead climb the crack on the right wall of the big groove for about 8m to a small spike which projects horizontally. It seems very solid, but handle it with care all the same.
From the top of the spike, step left into the bed of the groove and then out left again, using a dirty crack, to swing onto the rib. Climb the rib and a short v-groove to a stance below three large upright flakes.

3. (19m) Go between the middle and right-hand flakes and climb a large v-groove. Belay where it runs out into a broad grass slope littered with boulders.

4. (50m) – scrambling and walking. There are several ways up this broken middle section; the quickest is to walk up to the top left corner of the bouldery grass slope, where a trodden path leads into a short corner. Climb this corner, then step right and follow a path up and right for about 15m. Follow a boulder-strewn rock gangway leftwards, and then a couple of short grooves lead up to another broad sloping terrace.

Terrace Wall now looms just above, an unmistakable sweep of steep clean rock. Its grey buttresses provide some of the best and steepest VS rock climbs on Tryfan's East Face. Go up to the right to reach it and then back left along its base. It is possible to traverse off left all the way into

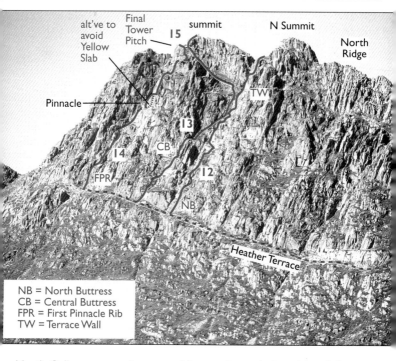

alt've to avoid Yellow Slab

Final Tower Pitch 15

summit

N Summit

North Ridge

Pinnacle

TW

13

CB

14

12

FPR

NB

Heather Terrace

NB = North Buttress
CB = Central Buttress
FPR = First Pinnacle Rib
TW = Terrace Wall

North Gully, or to continue scrambling up the rocks just right of the gully, but either of these would miss the best climbing on the route. Towards its left side, Terrace Wall leans back a little. An obvious feature here, at about half-height, is a large hanging block with a slash of quartz across its middle. Directly below this, just above ground level, is a bay with a rock ledge floor.

5. (30m) Step up onto the ledge flooring the bay. From its left end climb a left-slanting groove and continue in the same line over a series of flakes to a quartz ledge: this quartz is the leftward continuation of the slash on the hanging block, which can be seen on the right. Step left into a little groove, then left again onto a short rib, and climb this to a ledge. Belay just below a rough grey slab.

Spot the climbers high on the North Buttress

Tryfan East Face Expedition

6. (27m) Known for many years as The Traverse; the capitals may sound ominous, but this is a great pitch. However as on all traverses the leader should take care to protect the second, and some thought should also be given to minimising rope-drag.

Climb diagonally rightward across the grey slab. Before it steepens up, move horizontally right across some black mossy streaks, then go up and right to a vegetated ledge. From its right end step up then traverse to the right along a line of flakes, with accumulating exposure, to a large perched flake. Squeeze behind this, step down, and edge round a slight rib to reach a small rock ledge. From its right end go up a short groove, step right and then down again to continue the traverse to the clean horizontal plane of Belle Vue Terrace.

7. (16m) The wall behind the belay is quite steep but has good holds. Climb straight up for 10m then bear a little left to some big perched flakes. Step off the highest of these to pull over the final slight bulge. Scramble up a few metres to the modest summit of North Buttress.

Next: The North Ridge path is just metres away and can be followed – not entirely without interest! – left, to the summit or right, down to the valley. Perhaps a more fitting continuation is to scramble up to the North Peak and follow the ridge to Tryfan's main summit, keeping as close to the crest as possible.

To return to the foot of the face for another route, the best and most fitting descent is by Central Buttress, as described below, starting from the summit.

13. Central Buttress via Little and North Gullies (descent) Grade 1
Vertical height loss about 200m: guide time about 30 minutes

The best scrambling descent route from the top of Central Buttress back to Heather Terrace is via the upper section of North Gully and the deep runnel of Little Gully, which breaks through the right-hand (north) side of Central Buttress. Apart from a little scree, which is easily avoided, the rock is generally solid and clean, especially in the lower section, mainly due to its use by climbers as a descent route for climbs on Terrace Wall. The scramble starts from beside the obelisks of Adam and

Tryfan East Face Expedition

Eve and passes through some magnificent rock scenery. There are no escape options during the descent, apart from turning round and climbing back up to the summit.

Start between the twin pillars Adam and Eve. Descend polished rocks on the east side for a few metres, then scramble down a cracked slab on the south side (right, facing downhill). Follow worn boulders back round to the left to join a path, which meanders down several short rocky steps. Some of the moves are quite committing in exposed situations and care is needed in wet conditions. Below the steps follow the path north along a level section and descend a polished rocky corner. Continue along the path to gain the scree and grass terrace of the amphitheatre at the top of North Gully, just below the col between the Central and North summits.

Descend the wide scree and grass slopes of North Gully, avoiding some large mossy boulders by a zigzag descent down grassy slopes on the left (looking out). You suddenly arrive at a scree bay above a steep drop. The bay is overlooked by some slabs on Central Buttress and by the impressive Terrace Wall of North Buttress.

An obvious, well-worn ledge now leads off right (looking out) below the slabs of Central Buttress. Walk along the ledge, descend a rocky step, and continue down a path to a notch at the top of Little Gully. This is an excellent viewpoint out across the Ogwen Valley.

To get down into the trough of Little Gully, the first moves beside a large overhanging boulder are quite awkward, but easier scrambling soon follows down a series of steep rocky steps and corners. Although some of the descent is in the actual bed of the gully, the best scrambling is often down clean rock, well endowed with spiky holds, just outside the gully on the right (north side). Avoid the final awkward square-cut mossy section at the bottom of the gully by a rock ramp on the right wall (looking out). A scree slope now leads down to Heather Terrace at the point where the path is split by a large boulder.

14. First Pinnacle Rib 169m V. Diff If the Yellow Slab is avoided the route is Diff.
Guide time about 2 1/2 hours

Pinnacle Rib rivals Grooved Arete as the most popular route on Tryfan, and

few would dispute that it deserves it. The climbing is uncomplicatedly pleas-
urable, and there's plenty of time to relax on the commodious stances and
enjoy the view. But – and it is a sizeable but – the notorious Yellow Slab lies
in waiting above half-height.

Many a leader has approached this thinking, 'it can't be that hard', and
many have suffered embarrassment; for a few the consequences have
been considerably more painful. Always delicate, its holds have been polished by more than a century of shuffling feet and sweaty palms. It can
be avoided, but without it the route seems a little bloodless.

Above this the final pitches pass quickly and the route finishes close
to the summit of the mountain.

First climbed in 1894.

Approach: To reach the climb from the roadside, follow the directions
for North Buttress (Route 12 above) to the start of that route.
Continue along Heather Terrace, passing below North Gully (deeper
than its predecessors). Those who have descended Central Buttress will
emerge from Little Gully about 50m further on, where the path divides
around a large boulder. The path continues below Central Buttress, its
rocky base interrupted mid-way along by a wide bay of grass and
heather. Just to the right of this, FPR is scratched on the rock – just to
confuse you, as this as this is the start of Second Pinnacle Rib (a route
of similar standard, which converges with First Pinnacle Rib above the
Yellow Slab).

Continue past the bay until about 10m short of South Gully.

Start where FPR again appears, this time inscribed on the side of a van-
sized block, above which a clean slab runs up to some overhangs. And
this time you can believe it.

1. (18m) Gain the top of the van-sized block, using the crack on its left
and the rib just left again. Climb up to a large spike and then the open
groove above. Just below some overhangs, step right to a small sloping
ledge and nut belays.

2. (21m) Climb a pale open groove for 10m to a small recess. The continuation groove above is grassy, so step left onto a big spike and left
again onto the crest of the ridge. This eases all too soon into a big

canted platform, with nut belays in its top left corner.

3. (30m) Above is a broad groove almost filled by a big fin-like block. Climb the groove, keeping left of the block. Above is another large platform, a possible stance. Climb a groove/chimney in the next steep wall to reach yet another platform overlooking a large gully (South Gully) on the left.

4. (40m) Walk right 10m and climb an open chimney (take care with detached blocks). Scramble up past more potential stances to a 10m tower split by an open groove. Climb the groove or the face to its left: the face is better and harder, maybe a good warm-up for the Yellow Slab. Just above is a 5m step; belay at its top, just below the eponymous (and unmistakable) Pinnacle.

Scramble up to the gap behind the Pinnacle and regroup.

5. (15m) Directly behind the Pinnacle is the Yellow Slab. Once, no doubt, a sheer delight, it is now worn and raddled to the point of being Severe in boots. There's no sense of exposure but the difficulties don't ease until you are high enough to hurt yourself.

Climb the Slab's left edge to a sloping foot-shelf (it may be found a little easier to use the corner and set-back slab just to the left). Move right, to the base of a small hanging groove. All this demands trust in your feet, and is hard to protect, though a few small wires can be worried in. Once the groove is gained the holds steadily improve, though it's still a few moves to bombproof protection. If sacks (or seconds!) are being hauled, belay at the first small ledge just above the groove. Otherwise continue a few metres more to a larger ledge.

The whole thing can be avoided by walking 15m right and climbing an open groove slanting back left.

6. (22m) Just to the left, a curving groove-corner arcs up through sheaves of rock. Some of these are quite fragile and need careful handling. Where the groove pinches out just below the top, a step left onto the face makes life easier. Belay on a block-strewn grass ledge just above.

7. (23m) Continue up the ridge with no great difficulty until it ends at a fine balcony, with blocks to belay on just above.

Next: This is the official end of the route, but it's a shame to ignore the

Tryfan East Face Expedition

steep tower that looms above – the Final Wall. The dark corner cleft that splits it is Thomson's Chimney, a strenuous V.Diff, but a line further right, though contrived, is more in keeping with the climbing below.

15. Final Wall Pitch 23m Diff
Guide time about 15 minutes

1. (23m) Two obvious horizontal ledges break up the wall right of Thomson's Chimney. Climb the short steps below these. From the upper ledge climb a steep groove just a few metres left of the end of the wall. There's a tricky move before you can reach the excellent finishing holds.

Next: The final belay is within spitting distance of the walkers' path, which continues up left, winding round the final tower of the mountain to the summit.

Descents: Central Buttress is again available as a descent, but at the end of the day the South Ridge is the easiest and sunniest option. There is endless choice of ways through, over and around the chaos of huge boulders and rock steps. It's generally most satisfying to stick as close to the crest as possible.

As the ridge begins to spread out, various intermittent paths and lines of wear branch off rightwards, heading down into Cwm Bochlwyd. A little lower down is a level pause before the ridge makes one last rise to the little Far South Peak. From the stile in the gap a steep path descends to the southern (upper) end of Heather Terrace; as a possible way of returning to the foot of the East Face climbs this is longer and less interesting than the descent of Central Buttress. Continue over or round to right of the Far South Peak to Bwlch Tryfan, a good place for spotting wild goats.

From here, you have several options, including continuing on up to Glyder Fach by Bristly Ridge (Route 10). There's also a choice of descents. The one on the east side, into Cwm Tryfan, is rough and wearisome. Unless your next destination is the campsite at Gwern Gof Uchaf, it makes more sense to descend on the west side, into Cwm Bochlwyd. After the initial steepness the path descends gently alongside Llyn Bochlwyd, then more steeply again alongside a series of cascades.

Tryfan East Face Expedition

From below these, the main path bears left to Ogwen. Or, if you need to return to the foot of the North Ridge, branch off right here, passing below the steep little crag of Bochlwyd Buttress.

One final option, but the most fitting to complete an Alpine day, is to descend the North Ridge (Route 9), following the crest as closely as possible, and preferably descending the steep Grade 2 wall mentioned in the ascent description rather than the bouldery gully.

leaping Adam & Eve - the Freedom of Tryfan

Tryfan East Face Expedition

Y Glyderau

Y Glyderau – 'the Glyders' to generations of English-speaking climbers and walkers – can mean just the two peaks that bear the name, but usually refers more generally to the massive ridge of which they are the centrepiece. To the east this declines gradually towards Capel Curig, with lots of easy grassy going, and only a few minor crags disrupting its slopes. In the other direction, the ridge swings to roughly north-north-west, and while it sends monotonous slopes of tough sedge and grass down to the Llanberis valley, its east-facing cwms hold several more crags of interest to us.

Fittingly, it is the two eponymous peaks that are the main focus of climbing interest in the range, along with Tryfan (covered in the previous section) and the low-lying crags on the southern slope, above Llanberis Pass (in the next one). The Glyderau Fach and Fawr are virtual twins, with only five metres difference in height, and both showing a

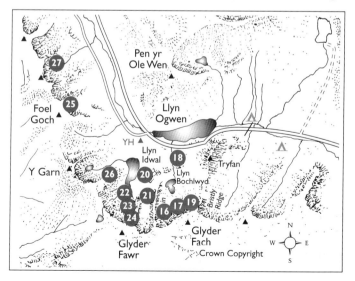

predominantly rocky aspect to the north; but in climbing terms they are quite distinctive.

At first glance, Glyder Fach is a shambles. In fact its crumbling aspect camouflages several buttresses of excellent steep rock with a good supply of positive holds. The climbing is quintessentially hearty and old-fashioned, making much use of cracks and corners, with only the Alphabet Slabs offering a note of open delicacy.

Glyder Fawr, on the other hand, has a straightforward architecture that is easily grasped. The clean lines of the Idwal Slabs set the tone, mirrored again and again in the higher crags. To the right and set further back is the inverted arch of Clogwyn y Geifr. Bisecting this is the gloomy gash of Twll Du, better known as the Devil's Kitchen.

Whether it's botanists drawn by the flora of Cwm Idwal, walkers heading for the heights, or fellow-climbers, there's usually plenty of company around. But peace can still be found in the deeper recesses. Even the Idwal Slabs can be quiet, if you start early enough; higher up, or on the cliffs of Glyder Fach, it's possible to be the only party in sight. Then you can begin to imagine what it was like for the nail-booted, tweed-jacketed, pipe-smoking climbers of legend.

Glyder Fach Crag Day

The main cliff of Glyder Fach is named, with total simplicity, as Main Cliff. It sits on the north west face of the mountain, high above Llyn Bochlwyd, occupying most of the space between Bristly Ridge (on the left, east side) and Y Gribin. With its sheer pillars and walls of grey rock split by cracks and corners, it's a complex and messy-looking area of rock that, surprisingly, hides a lot of good climbing. Most of the rock is very sound, rough and clean with good friction and large holds, allowing climbing in even poor weather conditions. However, on sunny, summer afternoons the rocks are warm and friendly. There are excellent routes of all grades to be found here.

The layout is best understood by studying the diagram. For now, we focus on the foot of the face, and the conspicuously smooth and clean Alphabet Slabs which carry our first route, Delta (the alphabet in question being the Greek one). Immediately to left of the Alphabet Slabs is the lowest part of Main Gully, and this provides a Grade 1 scrambling descent.

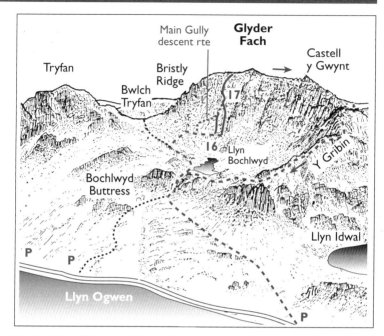

To the right of Alphabet Slabs is the conspicuous East Gully, running the full height of the cliff, but relatively narrow in its lower part. The buttress edge to its left forms East Gully Arete. Much further to the right is the wide West Gully, with its large scree fan below. Dolmen Ridge (Route 19) starts to right of this but crosses it below half-height to follow the buttress edge.

The Alphabet Slabs provide a number of excellent short climbs, which are in marked contrast to the steeper and more strenuous routes on nearby buttresses.

16. Delta 43m Difficult
Guide time: about 40 minutes

This is a pleasant route involving some balancy climbing up the Alphabet Slabs followed by an awkward crack.

Glyder Fach Crag Day

Approach is most often made from Ogwen Cottage. Follow the obvious path behind the toilet block. Take the main line on the left, not the branch which goes into a narrow rocky gorge. At the first big right-hand bend, after 7 or 8 minutes, bear slightly left onto a smaller but still clear path. Follow this, gently ascending over open slopes and then up more steeply alongside a series of cascades.

Glyder Fach

East Gully Continuation

Descent route (Main Gully)

East Gully Arete

Delta

17

16

Above these Llyn Bochlwyd is soon reached, and a choice: which way round the lake? The right-hand (west) way is shorter, and with care you can keep to grass for most of it. But to throw a few extra bits of scrambling into the mix, go round the left side and up some conspicuous clean light-coloured rocks below and left of the East Buttress. Traverse to the right along its base (by traversing left instead, this is also a possible and crowd-free approach to Bristly Ridge).

It is of course easy to incorporate Bochlwyd Buttress (Route 18) in the approach. Alternatively, strong goers may fancy a route on Tryfan first, descending the south ridge to Bwlch Tryfan and then contouring almost horizontally right to the crag.

Start 1m left of a grassy runnel bounding the right side of the Alphabet Slabs. A shallow circular scoop is directly above.

1. (21m) Climb delicately up left for 9m to reach a small ledge just below the shallow, circular scoop. Just left of the scoop is a crack, which is awkward to reach. Climb this, with good runners, to a ledge and good wire belays in a crack.

Glyder Fach Crag Day

2. (22m) From the ledge climb easy-angled slabs and ledges up to the quartz-speckled terrace at the top of Alphabet Slabs.

Descent: Head left along the terrace to scramble down Main Gully on loose rock, ledges and (at the bottom) slabs.

Next: Follow the undulating path a short distance to the right, past the foot of the route just climbed and along the base of the cliff to the foot of the deep, dark cleft of East Gully.

17. East Gully Arete 138m Difficult
Guide time: About 3 hours

A long, varied route and a good introductory climb for beginners, with a real mountaineering feel about it. It is a route of two characters: up to the terrace that crosses the top of the Alphabet Slabs the climbing is steep and exposed, then it becomes an easy ridge. Despite this it is a continuous and natural line.

Start at a steep wall just left of the bottom of East Gully. At the base of the wall is a pedestal with a quartz block at its foot.

1. (15m) Climb up left of the quartz block to the top of the pedestal. Avoid the steep wall in front of you by moving right, almost into the gully, then climb up the edge next to the gully, before returning left to a small ledge. Continue up past a band of quartz to a good belay ledge.

2. (23m) From a bollard step right and climb up delicate slabs beside the edge of East Gully. At about 9m climb a flake crack leading to a ledge and rocky bay below a slab. Climb up the slab by an awkward groove to a sloping platform at the foot of a long ridge. This stance is at the right end of the terrace which crosses above the Alphabet Slabs; the ridge above will form the upper part of the route.

3. (45m) Start up the ridge by climbing the steep right edge of a short, rocky rib overlooking East Gully. The holds are good and the rock has excellent friction. This leads in about 15m to a prominent notch. Ahead are two ribs separated by a narrow grassy gully. Climb the left rib on

Glyder Fach Crag Day

Glyder Fach Crag Day

opposite page: Sally Inglis on the first pitch of East Gully Arete

excellent holds and with numerous runners for 30m to a level rocky area with good block belays.

4. (10m) Scramble up some piled blocks to a rocky ledge at the foot of a more compact and steeper section of rock. Good block belay.

5. (30m) Scramble up easy rock for a few metres, then climb an obvious short narrow crack. A spike at the crack's top provides a good runner; then mantelshelf onto the spike itself. Step delicately up to the left and climb up a few metres (difficult but well protected) to a narrow rock ledge. Continue up easier rock to block belays in another notch.

6. (15m) Cross the notch and follow the easy ridge which curves left to overlook Main Gully, then continues over piles of more blocks to join open rocky slopes.

Descent: If you wish to return directly to the foot of the face, descend the well-worn rocks in the rocky depression of Main Gully (a Grade 1 scramble). The hardest moves involve bypassing a chockstone near the bottom of the gully. The gully emerges onto the left end of the terrace at the top of the Alphabet Slabs. From the terrace scramble down Main Gully on loose rock, ledges and (at the bottom) slabs.

And now? From the top of the climb, open rocky slopes lead up to the summit of Glyder Fach. From there you can either descend Bristly Ridge (Route 10 backwards) or walk west over Castell y Gwynt and scramble easily down Y Gribin back to Llyn Bochlwyd (Route 10's continuation).

For a longer round, you could continue over Glyder Fawr and descend from Llyn y Cwn down the side of the Devil's Kitchen into Cwm Idwal. The path crosses below Idwal Slabs and provides a close look at the start of the various routes up the slabs.

Other recommended routes on the Main Face include the challenging and aptly named Chasm Route (85m V. Diff), a real old-fashioned climb involving some thrutchy cracks and chimneys, and the more delicate Slab Route (73m V. Diff), both on the East Buttress to the left of Main Gully. While to the right of East Gully, on Hawk's Nest Buttress, is the fascinating Needle's Eye Climb (58m V. Diff), the exciting part involving a squeeze through a smooth crack into a cave, the Needle's Eye.

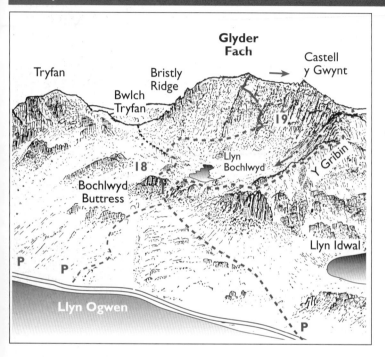

Glyder Fach Expedition
186m climbing/scrambling: up to Diff

Having identified the Alphabet Slabs and East Buttress, the eye is even more ready to dismiss the rest of the north face of Glyder Fach as broken and sprawling, unworthy of further attention. But there is much more good rock to be found. Dolmen Ridge is a fine choice, climbing the full height of the cliff. If not quite Alpine in scale, it certainly is Alpine in its mix of scrambling and roped climbing.

A route on the cheery little Bochlwyd Buttress is a great way to liven up the approach. It lacks the forbidding atmosphere, but Arete and Slab is technically a notch harder than anything on Dolmen Ridge and this makes it a great confidence-booster.

Bochlwyd Buttress

18. Arete and Slab, Bochlwyd Buttress 36m Diff
Guide time about 1 hour

A grand little climb that packs a lot in. The steep crack of the first pitch contrasts with more open, delicate climbing higher up. First climbed in 1927.

Approach is most often made from Ogwen Cottage. Follow the obvious path behind the toilet block. Take the main line on the left, not the branch which goes into a narrow rocky gorge. At the first big right-hand bend, after 7 or 8 minutes, bear slightly left onto a smaller but still clear path. Follow this, gently ascending over open slopes. Where the slope steepens ahead, a series of cascades can be seen just ahead; a short way further left is a small steep crag. This is Bochlwyd Buttress. Cross the stream just below the cascades and go up a rougher slope to the base of the crag.

The crag can also be reached from the lay-by (SH659602) about

Glyder Fach Expedition

halfway along Llyn Ogwen, on the south side of the road, opposite a boulder-strewn promontary. At the west end of the lay-by a stile, steps and eroded paths lead up steep ground to gentler slopes. The path promptly becomes harder to follow, but the crag is now visible.

Start at the extreme right end of the front face of the crag. The bounding arete is split by a deep wide crack, almost a chimney.

1. (18m) Climb the crack, with a steep entry. Take care with one or two suspect flakes. At the top of the crack pull out left onto a ledge on the front face. Move to its left end to belay.

2. (6m) Climb a short steep wall on the left and move up to a large sloping ledge.

3. (12m) A tricky move out left onto an exposed slab can slow progress for some time. Once the commitment is made, the slab itself is more straightforward and soon leads up to the crest of the buttress.

Next: Scramble up and left to reach a smooth slab, somewhat reminiscent of Tryfan Fach, for which it's probably worth staying roped. It's about 10m high and Diff in standard. Or, to save time, scramble up the more broken rocks on its right. Continue straight up the hillside, with more outcrops that can be avoided or included at will, until the slope levels off. Glyder Fach appears ahead and in a few more strides Llyn Bochlwyd appears just below.

19. Dolmen Ridge Moderate (mostly Grade 2 scrambling)
Vertical height about 150 metres: guide time about 2 hours

A great high mountain scramble; it feels quite wild and remote yet the approach is reasonable. Although described in other books as a scramble, the key pitch is steep, exposed, and tricky enough to demand a rope and at least a few runners.

There's a scrappy start on the wrong side of the gully but then comes a dramatic change when it breaks out onto Dolmen Buttress. The pitch up this, though well supplied with holds, is steep and exposed. This is climbing, not scrambling. Above this the ridge has an Alpine flavour and

makes a direct line to the summit. The rock is generally clean, though not always sound.

Approach: If not tackling Bochlwyd Buttress first, then either of the approaches given for that crag leads also to a steep path alongside cascades about 50m to the right of the buttress.

On reaching Llyn Bochlwyd there is a choice: which way round the lake? The right-hand (west) way is shorter, and with care you can keep to grass for most of it. But to throw a few extra bits of scrambling into the mix, go round the left side and up some conspicuous clean light-coloured rocks below and left of the East Buttress. Traverse to the right along its base (by traversing left instead, this is also a possible and crowd-free approach to Bristly Ridge).

Useful landmarks are the small clean Alphabet Slab and East Gully above it, to the right of the East Buttress. Further right, another large

Glyder Fach Expedition

Glyder Fach Expedition

Bernie Carer on the upper section of the Dolmen Ridge

gully cuts through the crags. Guidebooks variously name this as West or Central Gully. As there isn't another gully to its right, West Gully seems the more logical name. A broad scree fan spilling from it helps to identify it conclusively.

Start at the base of the rocks immediately right of West Gully, where a slender band of quartz slants up to the right. Looking up, Dolmen Buttress appears as a steep tower high above, to the left of the gully. But first we have to get there, and this is a little devious.

Go up and right via quartzy steps to a blocky rib: though vague, it is the best line hereabouts.

From a grass patch at the rib's top go diagonally right on crisp flakes for a few metres then back left on quartz to ledges below a steeper wall. Follow a narrow path horizontally left below the wall to a rib just right of the gully. Climb the rib until it peters out in an area of more broken rock, an extension of the gully bed. There's much loose stuff hereabouts. No line is obviously better than another and all lead to an amphitheatre, dominated by the near-vertical Dolmen Buttress on the left.

Traverse nervously left across the gully and then carefully along ledges to gain a broad, almost horizontal, ramp which runs upwards and to the left below the steep amphitheatre face of Dolmen Buttress. At the ramp's far end a bridged block makes a good belay for what follows.

1. (27m) Climb a short groove immediately above the block and make a very awkward move up past a sharp spike into a second groove above. At its top climb an open corner above, finishing on either side wall, to a ledge with good belays.

A much easier section of about a rope-length – and it is worth staying roped – leads to the base of another steep tower with a large table-like block perched conspicuously high up. Climb up aiming just to right of the block: a tricky step half-way is the reason you kept the rope on. Move left to pass behind the block and keep traversing left below another perched block. Climb a dirty groove, awkward to enter, break out left just below its top, then climb straight up to regain the crest, now much more broken.

There follows an easy section with many options, but blocks are often precariously balanced. The ridge kinks right to a small col at the head of West Gully. A final short steep section above soon tails back into the main mass of Glyder Fach, and the summit rockpile appears dead ahead.

Next: There's more fun to be had among the jumble of massive blocks and flakes forming the summit area, among them the famous and photogenic Cantilever. From the summit follow the ridge, slightly south of west, over or round Castell y Gwynt. Cross the col beyond – Bwlch y Ddwy-glyder – and then swing right onto the Gribin Ridge which is followed down to Llyn Bochlwyd. All this is described in more detail under Route 10.

Cneifion Expedition
240m climbing/scrambling: up to V.Diff

Despite its proximity to both Cwm Idwal and the popular Devil's Kitchen footpath, the wonderful hanging valley of Cwm Cneifion remains seldom-trod. It's easily visible from above; from either the main Glyder Ridge which forms its headwall, or from the subsidiary ridges of Y Gribin and Seniors' Ridge, which provide its steep and craggy sides.

Glyder Fach Expedition

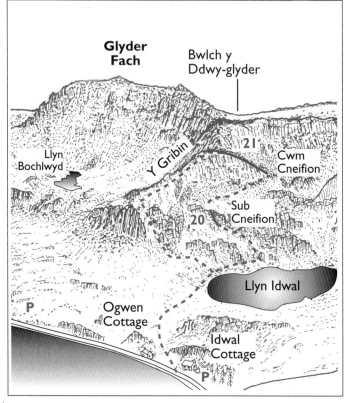

Cneifion Expedition

The Cneifion Arete is the only climbable feature but what a gem: awesome and Alpine yet surprisingly easy.

To call this the Cneifion Expedition is perhaps to stretch the geography, as the Sub-Cneifion Rib, on which the day starts out, isn't in Cwm Cneifion at all but is a rocky outcrop above Cwm Idwal. This is a technicality however, as the rib, which makes a wonderful outing in its own right, provides the perfect hors d'oeuvre for the day's activities, offering the initial knee-up for a spectacular 'valley-floor to mountain-summit' day out.

20. Sub Cneifion Rib 110m V. Diff
Guide time 3 1/2 hours

The Sub Cneifion Rib is often deserted when the other Ogwen crags are teeming with climbers. It offers exceptionally good climbing throughout its length; but the hardest moves and the finest positions come near the top, where a daunting looking nose is turned on good holds above a big drop. First climbed by J. Menlove Edwards back in 1931, it leaves you in the perfect position to continue into Cwm Cneifion.

Approach: From Idwal Cottage, follow the main path that leads up from the left of the toilet block. Continue to a gate next to a small island in Llyn Idwal on your right and turn left to walk uphill, with the wall to your left. After 10m, turn right onto a faint path that leads up towards the top of a grassy hill. At this stage you can't see the rib, although it's almost directly ahead and uphill slightly. Once it does come into sight, walk towards it and then continue to the right around its foot for 50m until you reach a huge boulder, a metre out from the rib. A few paces further on, a flake points skywards.

Start directly behind the flake, with a distinctive corner 3m to the right. The rock on the slabby rib above is visibly clean and climbed, and the ground below the route is well worn.

1. (15m) Climb the rocky skirt onto the distinctive slabby rib and follow it for a few moves to a crack. Now move slightly to the left and follow a double crack to a corner, where the rock steepens. Climb straight up this steep corner to its top and move slightly left, on good holds, to a cramped belay ledge.

2. (15m) Head straight up from the stance on slabby rock and then bear left to climb around a large bulge. The climbing gets easier here as you continue up over broken rocks to a large flake that makes a perfect sling belay.

3. (15m) Now scramble easily up and leftwards over heathery ledges to gain a very easy-angled rib with a steep drop to the left. Climb this rib

Cneifion Expedition

Gribin Ridge

20

to Cneifion Arete

Sub Cneifion Rib

from
Ogwen
Cottage

Cneifion Expedition

for 5m to a good stance on the left, beneath a steeper section with a right facing corner.

4. (15m) Scramble right, back across the rib, and down onto a patch of rough grassy ground. Cross this to the right, to reach the foot of another clean rib of easy-angled rock. Continue up a few metres to a saucer-like ledge at the foot of a steep nose of rock. There are plenty of belay options here.

5. (35m) This is the crux pitch, with a few difficult and strenuous moves. Climb awkwardly onto the steep nose and then traverse around to the right, to where a diagonally slanting line of small holds leads back up left. The moves become awkward but there are plenty of small foot placements to assist in reaching the crest above the steep nose. Now climb the cracked bulge above to a small platform beneath a broken wall.

There are placements for a belay in the broken wall.

6. (15m) Continue directly up the broken wall to another grassy platform. Beyond this is an exposed but easy-angled rib that leads to the top.

Next: a clear path runs across the top of the climb. Turn right onto this and walk up into the cwm, which is absolutely stunning. Continue up the valley, with stream on your right, and you'll soon make out the pronounced arete, ahead and on the left. From the grassy valley floor, a scree path leads to the foot of the climb.

21. Cneifion Arete 130m Mod
Guide time 1 1/2 hours

It may look daunting from below but there's little to worry about on this wonderful climb/scramble that traces a very airy line up the steep nose of the arete and then follows a knife-edge crest onto Y Gribin. The first few moves are without a doubt the hardest, but even they can be turned easily enough if you keep your eyes open. Most of the ridge above could be climbed moving together, stopping to take belays wherever the not inconsiderable exposure may suggest.

This truly classic arete was first scaled in 1905 by G. Barlow and Miss E. Clark.

Start a metre or so to the right of the foot of the arete.

1. (25m) Technically, this is the hardest pitch of the route. Follow a shallow groove up the right face of the arete for a few metres until the way is blocked by some obstructing pinnacles. These are most easily passed on the right. Move back left above them to gain the arete crest and continue as close to the crest as possible until the terrain eases at the foot of a deep and awkward chimney. Belay here, beneath the chimney, where communication will still be easy.

2. (10m) Now climb the chimney, using holds on both sides. This leads back on to the crest of the arete where it's possible to belay.
The route continues as a scramble.

Cneifion Expedition

Cneifion Expedition

Y Gribin

21

Cneifion Arete

from Sub Cneifion

Keep the rope handy, possibly even moving together, and keep as close to the true arete as you dare. Most of the tricky stuff is avoidable down to the left but the ridge does narrow one last time and, although the holds are excellent, you may choose to belay across this section. From here, continue easily onto Y Gribin, where you'll meet a path.

To descend, you could turn left onto this path and follow it steeply down to a junction of paths, where you turn left to follow a wall back to Llyn Idwal.

And now? Alternatively, make your climb into a mountain climb. Bear right and head up the Gribin ridge, not on the path but on the crest, up left, which is a scramble at just Grade 1 with a couple of exposed moments. At its top you'll see the summit of Glyder Fawr just over to the right. To descend from this, drop to the west on a steep scree path to Llyn y Cwn.

Just to right of the lake you'll find the top of the Devil's Kitchen path. Turn right onto this and follow it down, to pass beneath the Idwal Slabs to Llyn Idwal and the car park. Another option from Llyn y Cwn is to carry on up to Y Garn and follow the down scramble of Route 26.

Trevor Gunner on the Cneifion Arete

Cneifion Expedition

Glyder Fawr Expedition
550m climbing/scrambling: up to V. Diff

If the ideal for an expedition is to get from valley to summit on rock all the way, then they don't come much better than this. Admittedly there is an opening walk, but it is easy and mostly level, and in the later stages alongside Llyn Idwal the full itinerary can be seen ahead. Despite its crowded familiarity, this never fails to impress as a grand mountain spectacle, with its inverted arch of strata centred on the ugly cleft of the Devil's Kitchen. A great sweep of ribs and slabs fans out up to the left, and these are the target of the day's endeavours.

The Idwal Slabs are usually busy, but their popularity is fully deserved and it is a place of such strong character that the crowds are rarely oppressive. And as soon as you leave the slabs behind, it's possible you won't meet another person until the summit slopes of Glyder Fawr. It's such contrasts that make this a truly rounded mountain day.

The Idwal Slabs have very clean, indeed polished, rock but the upper stages carry much less traffic. Accordingly, the rock higher up is rougher, but generally still clean. In dubious conditions it's possible to bypass Central Arete and follow the easier Seniors' Ridge all the way to the summit plateau.

22. Ordinary Route (Idwal Slabs) 131m Moderate
Guide time about 1 1/2 hours

This is the easiest route on the main slab and there's relatively little of the tiptoe slab climbing for which the crag is renowned. In fact it is a more varied route than its more prestigious neighbours, thoroughly worthwhile in its own right and ideal for a brisk start to a long day.

First climbed in 1897.

Approach: From Ogwen Cottage, follow the obvious path behind the toilet block. Take the 'main line' on the left, not the branch which goes into a narrow rocky gorge. At the first big right-hand bend, after 7 or 8 minutes, you'll pass a smaller path branching left, heading for Llyn Bochlwyd. The main path, still blindingly obvious, passes under the long low crag of Clogwyn y Tarw, more usually known as the Gribin Facet, and leads quickly to the shores of Llyn Idwal. Bear left, still following the

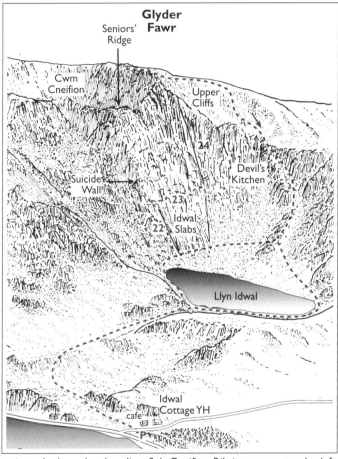

Glyder
Fawr

Seniors'
Ridge

Cwm
Cneifion

Upper
Cliffs

24

Devil's
Kitchen

Suicide
Wall

23

22 Idwal
Slabs

Llyn Idwal

Idwal
Cottage YH

cafe

P

Glyder Fawr Expedition

main path along the shoreline. Sub-Cneifion Rib is seen up on the left before the path makes a slight climb to the skinned ground at the foot of the Slabs.

Start: Just 3 metres right of the bottom left corner of the main slab is the start of the long crack-groove that runs right up the Slabs and defines this route. Seen from the crag foot it appears straight at first, then curving slightly to the right just before it disappears over the sky-line. A further landmark is a heather-filled groove a couple of metres further right.

1. (45m) Go straight up the crack to the beginning of the rightward bend. Climb over a block. There's a niche just above and a good ledge just above again. Belay on this ledge.

2. (30m) Cracks rise from both ends of the ledge. It's probably easiest to take the right hand one for about 4m to a spike runner, then traverse delicately left into the other. Continue straight up this until it widens into a scoop (possible belay). Continue up the crack for about 5m to a small ledge.

3. (36m) Climb easily straight up the continuation crack to a very noticeable steepening. Step up and right across a short mossy corner. Make a move up and then climb diagonally right to an excellent ledge.

4. (20m) Climb the short corner crack behind the belay (the wall on the right is easier but unprotected). Now make a rising leftward traverse, below a steeper bit of wall, round into a grassy bay near a prominent flat boulder.

Next: The plan may be to continue upward, or you may need, or choose, to descend from here. This is no laughing matter and certainly needs a detailed description. The first stage is the same whether you are descending or continuing on up. Either way, you'll need the rope again before too long. There is a third alternative, to continue upwards by scrambling, on Seniors' Ridge (Grade 1).

For all three continuations scramble up grass ledges and short steps to the terrace below the steeper rock of Holly Tree Wall, identified by a flat perched boulder. Since the easiest route on this is a good Severe, we need to bypass it and in fact the route gives it a wide berth to the left. From the terrace, a worn path leads off to the left, generally upward, over ledges and short steps. Watch for arrows scratched on the rock.

The path reaches a larger, roughly level, grass terrace, about level with the top of Holly Tree Wall. A steep smooth little buttress, about 10m

Glyder Fawr Expedition

Glyder
Fawr

Seniors
Ridge

Upper
Cliffs

Central
Arete
Direct

24

quartz ledge

The Arete 23

Suicide
Wall

Holly Tree
Wall

flat boulder on top
of ordinary route

Ordinary Route

22 Idwal
Slabs

high, above the right end of the terrace helps to identify the spot. The
direct descent, and the easier continuation by Seniors' Ridge, now part
company with the main route towards the Arete. The path continues
horizontally left from the left end of the steep smooth buttress mentioned above. Follow the path, well-worn rock, and a few scratched
arrows, up and left for another 50 metres. At the end 'way off' is

Glyder Fawr Expedition

scratched on the rock. Just beyond this the rock drops off abruptly into a steep gully.

Descent from the Slabs

It's vital to be sure you have correctly identified this point. Trying to descend anywhere else could get you into very serious trouble! The correct line down into the gully is obvious and well used. It is not as difficult as it looks but it is steep, polished and quite awkward. If you kept the rope on after Ordinary Route, you'll be glad of it now. If you took it off, it is advisable to put it back on here. It can be run over a rounded spike to protect the last one down.

The rest of the descent is much easier, an obvious eroded line running down below the very steep Suicide Wall. Some awkward steps can be avoided by moving right, away from the wall, and out onto easier grass slopes. If you don't need to return to the base of the Slabs, a narrow but distinct path branching off right makes for an easy descent, gently angling down to join the main path half way along Llyn Idwal.

Easier upwards option: Seniors' Ridge Grade 1

Rather than the V. Diff climb on The Arete, you may prefer to continue upwards by scrambling on Seniors' Ridge. From the top of the Slabs descent – the point where 'way off' is scratched on the rock – this trends back rightwards over a series of short walls and grass ledges. The ridge soon broadens out and becomes less steep. Its upper section gives a long easy scramble to the summit plateau of Glyder Fawr.

Continuing main route towards The Arete

The ascent towards The Arete continues from the terrace level with the top of Holly Tree Wall. The wall above the terrace shows a distinct grassy/rocky groove that runs up its centre onto a rightward trending ledge. Follow this groove to a boulder perched on the rightward trending ledge and then continue along the ledge for a few more metres to the foot of The Arete. The arete is actually more of a blunt prow but is easily recognised even from a distance by its clean grey face and, upon closer inspection, by a 3m band of quartz at its foot and by a leftward facing corner that marks its right-hand edge.

Left: Bernie Carter on Pitch 4, Idwal Slabs Ordinary Route

Glyder Fawr Expedition

23. The Arete 24m V. Diff
Guide time 40 mins

A wonderful clean line that offers some splendidly exposed positions high above Cwm Idwal. First climbed in 1929, this route is technically high in its grade as well as fairly thin on protection, making it one of the hardest routes in the whole book.

Start to the right of the arete, directly beneath the leftward facing corner.

1. (24m) Climb directly upwards for about 3m to the top of a flake that rests against the corner. Now trend leftwards along a line of small slab-by ledges that lead out onto the arete itself. The rest of the climb simply follows the arete upwards to its top.

Next follow a long scrambly traverse to the foot of the Upper Cliffs of Glyder Fawr. First move rightwards and upwards through a number of short rock bands and grassy terraces until, after approximately 30m, you pass a large flake leaning against a slab. Keep this to your left and continue up a shallow gully decorated with a few rock spikes until you reach a large boulder on your right. Continue for another 10m to a huge grassy terrace, bounded by quartzy ledges.

Follow a faint path to the right, along the ledge. This terminates on a boulder-strewn grassy slope that rises upwards towards the foot of the Upper Cliffs. It's best to get a good look at the cliffs from here and, in particular, identify the two distinctive gullies that cut through them. The left-hand one is East Gully. The right-hand one is known as Central Gully and the next climb, Central Arete, starts to the right of it.

Head upwards now, following a steep grassy ramp between rocky outcrops, until you reach the foot of the cliffs. Now turn right and walk along their base, passing beneath East and Central Gullies and continuing below the foot of a tall and slender grassy rake, to the foot of the next rocky rib, which is Central Arete.

24. Central Arete Direct 200m V. Diff
guide time: 3 1/2 hours

From a distance, the Upper Cliffs look daunting, but up close they provide some user-friendly low-grade rock climbs, the finest of which is Central Arete Direct – a North Wales mountaineering classic. First scaled in 1909 by a four-man team, it punches hard for its weight with a testing mid section that's followed by a ridge studded with spectacular gendarmes and Alpine-style spikes. Check your watch before starting, many parties have found themselves a few pitches short of the full climb as darkness falls.

Start 10m to the right of the very foot of the arete, on a well-trodden ledge.

1. (40m) The first pitch lacks any real coherence and can be scrambled. Climb directly up from the start, keeping as far left as possible to find clean rock. This section terminates on a good grassy ledge beneath a clean nose, marked with the initials CA on the rock.

2. (45m) Head straight up the arete on slabby rock that's a lot steeper than it appears. Continue for almost a whole rope-length to a good ledge (1m by 2m) in a corner to the right of the crest line. A flake provides nut and sling placements.

3. (15m) Return to the arete and continue on good holds for a few metres to the foot of a steeper section. Climb this, still up the arete crest, and follow more excellent holds to a ledge beneath a final steep section. Belay from rock spikes.

4. (100m) Climb straight up from the stance and follow the arete as it gradually levels off, leaving you with a series of pinnacles and gendarmes to surmount. Belay at any convenient point and then continue either without the rope or moving together until the ridges terminates on the rough bouldery slopes of the summit.

And Now: The summit of Glyder Fawr is a few minutes' walk away. From there, bear right to descend to Llyn y Cwn and turn right to follow the Devil's Ladder footpath back into Cwm Idwal.

Alternatively, thunder on up Y Garn to the Grade 2 descent of its East Ridge (Route 26).

Glyder Fawr Expedition

Foel Goch and Y Garn Expedition
Total scrambling 740m: maximum grade 2

There's more to the Glyderau than the eponymous twin peaks; the ridge continbues north-west over Y Garn and Foel Goch. These peaks have smoother outlines than Glyder Fawr or Tryfan; at first glance they offer fine ridge walking rather than scrambling or climbing. The ridge walking is there but so too are some fine crags, cwms and ridges, with the added attraction that solitude is often to be found – though the proximity of the A5 makes silence less likely. Y Garn's main ridges, overlooking Cwm Idwal, have more than a hint of the Alpine, while Creigiau Gleision, on Foel Goch, is a uniquely raddled wreck of a crag, forlorn and neglected.

It may strike some people as perverse to take the short route up and the longer one down again. But consider this: the art of climbing down is unfairly neglected, but sooner or later every mountaineer needs to do it. Then again, walking downhill is just as tiring as going up: any

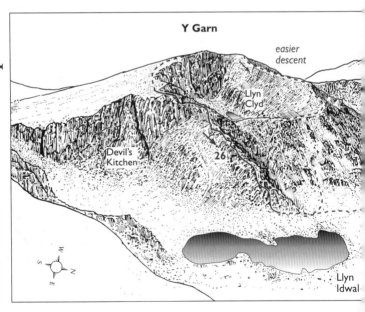

long-distance fell-runner will tell you that they use the uphill bits to rest. The best line on the Mushroom Garden is elusive in ascent and likely to evade you altogether in descent. If none of these arguments convince, feel free to read the description upside down and take the itinerary backwards!

25. The Mushroom Garden Grade 2 as described but all difficulties are easily avoided
Vertical height about 100 metres: guide time about 30 minutes

Were the Victorians into magic mushrooms? There's a hallucinogenic quality about Creigiau Gleision, which sprawls across the north-east flank of Foel Goch like an opium-smoker on a divan. This is not so much an expedition or a crag day as a trip... On a misty day the countless towers and twisted pinnacles become oppressive, even threatening, but on a sunny afternoon, with clear views down Nant Ffrancon to Anglesey and the sea, it's just the place for a leisurely jaunt. In season, the harvest will be, not mushrooms, but bilberries.

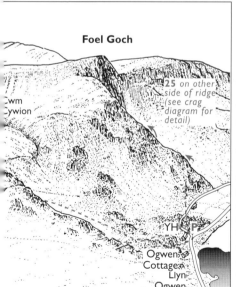

Foel Goch

25 on other side of ridge (see crag diagram for detail)

Cwm Cywion

YH   P

Ogwen Cottage

Llyn Ogwen

Approach: From Ogwen Cottage, follow the old road westward and mostly descending, past the youth hostel to a stone bridge. Immediately after this slant left up the slope on a faint path almost hidden by bracken. The path doesn't get any easier to follow, but keep heading up in the same general direction, crossing an old wire fence and then a dilapidated stone wall.

Foel Goch & Y Garn Expedition

Foel Goch

Creigiau Gleision

25

Follow sheep tracks just above the wall and then up more steeply, to pass above a small pale-coloured crag. Keep following the wall up a very steep bilberry slope until a traversing path is met. This leads easily round to the right into Cwm-coch. As it swings into the cwm a gully can be seen above, with a scree chute spilling from it. Masses of pinnacled rock rise to either side.

Start at the foot of the gully, on the right of the scree.
Climb the steep slope flanking the scree and continue on bilberry and easy rock until the first steep rock tower forces you into the gully bed. Climb straight up the gully for 30m to a slabby rock step and a path cutting across the gully.

The more formidable scramble of Needle's Eye Arete can be reached by moving up right to the narrow col behind a shark's fin, but for an easier life go up left to a corresponding col, and through it onto an open slope of scree and scattered outcrops.

Turn directly uphill again over a couple of short steps to a steeper barrier with a depression up its centre. Gain the depression by a nice little gangway slanting up from the right. Continue up the depression, or

Foel Goch & Y Garn Expedition

Bernie Carter high up on the Mushroom Garden scramble (Route 25), Foel Goch. Pen yr Ole Wen forms the backdrop.

climb the shattered little ridges on either side. These come together to form a better-defined ridge overlooking the gully on the right. Climb a step to a little notch, than a left-slanting slab leads up to grass below another steeper tower.

Skirt this tower on its left side by following a green traverse into a broad open gully. Keep to the gully's right hand side using as much rock as possible. A few more easy rocks lead out to a broad grassy shoulder. The rest is walking, but with some more impressive views of the tortuous gullies and pinnacles. When the main ridge is reached the summit of Foel Goch is a few minutes away up to the right.

Next: From the summit, there are several options. Least favoured is any attempt to descend the steep, vegetated ridge of Yr Esgair, despite its compelling line dropping from the summit. Severe health warnings apply! The best mountaineering plan is to follow the ridge to Y Garn. If this is too energetic on a hot day then from the col between Foel Goch and Y Garn a steep but simple slope leads down left into the silent, trackless Cwm Cywion.

Foel Goch & Y Garn Expedition

It is much better to climb Y Garn and then descend one of its ridges – the best of them, the East Ridge, is described next. The right-hand or western ridge is much more amenable for walkers – though still steep – and is a very popular way up or down Y Garn.

26. East Ridge of Y Garn (Descent) Grade 2
Vertical Height about 640m; Descent time about 2 hours.

Y Garn is an elegant mountain that dominates the Ogwen Valley in the shape of a comfortable armchair overlooking Llyn Idwal. Two fine curving ridges – the arms of the chair – sweep down to enclose a hanging cwm, Cwm Clyd, carved out by glacial action and containing a couple of exquisite lakes known by the single name of Llyn Clyd; this place is one of the hidden gems of Ogwen.

The west ridge, as mentioned above, is the walkers' route. The east ridge (right-hand looking down) descends as a grassy spur at first, until interrupted by the crag Castell y Geifr (Castle of the Goat). Though it's only about 80m high, it involves some exhilarating scrambling on its east (right, facing downhill) side. On wet and windy days it's best avoided. The most difficult and exposed section is a steep wall made up of a series of grey-coloured stacked blocks that rears above a connecting neck of rock. The broad lower section of the ridge offers easy scrambling marred by some loose rock.

Start: From the summit of Y Garn follow the east rim of Cwm Clyd and then descend scree and grass slopes to arrive at some boulders at the top of Castell y Geifr.

Directly below is a rocky corner holding some huge fallen boulders: scramble down these. Below this is a steep wall made up of stacked grey columnar blocks. Down below you can see the narrow neck of rock you are aiming for. Using the sharp edges of the enormous blocks climb carefully down the edge on the left side (looking out) in a fairly exposed position, getting harder as you go down. Below the stacked blocks, descend a short corner on well-scratched holds to a grassy bay. Climb down a short cracked wall, using the top of a flake for handholds, to arrive at the almost level connecting neck of rock about 25m down from the top of the steep wall of grey blocks.

Walk airily along the neck of rock, which is about 15m long, and

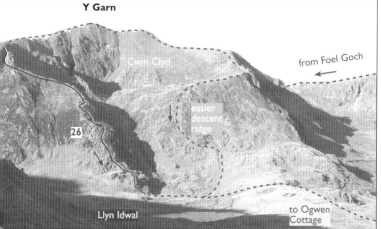

Y Garn

from Foel Goch ←

Cwm Clyd

easier
descent
ridge

26

Llyn Idwal

to Ogwen
Cottage

involves descending a short polished rocky step with good holds about halfway across. Beyond the neck continue down an easy rocky ridge for about 15m. The broken slabby rocks directly below lead to dangerous ground with a steep drop over a cliff. Avoid this by descending right (looking out) and scramble down a steep broken gully on fairly good holds for about 30m to scree slopes and the end of all difficulties.

From here you can relax and appreciate the view across Llyn Idwal to Tryfan, down Nant Ffrancon, and across to the pyramid-shaped Pen yr Ole Wen. Follow a footpath down the scree and round left to the base of the steep triangular buttress that you would have fallen over if you'd kept straight down the ridge. From the boulder field below the cliff follow a path down bilberry-covered slopes and then along a narrow ridge.

You could now descend rocky slopes left (north) into Cwm Clyd and follow a footpath alongside the stream from Llyn Clyd down into Cwm Idwal – a way that's quicker and prettier but misses out some interesting scrambling. Longer but more in keeping with the top section of the route is to continue along a faint path following the crest of the ridge, weaving around a series of short outcrops. When the ridge broadens pick a line down between rocky outcrops separated by grass and heather terraces. The easiest ways are usually found on the right-hand

Foel Goch & Y Garn Expedition

Foel Goch & Y Garn Expedition

Steep scrambling on the East Ridge of Y Garn

(eastern) flanks of the outcrops overlooking Llyn Idwal. At the foot of the ridge, bear left to cross a stream from Llyn Clyd, and then contour across grassy slopes to join a broad path at the bottom of Y Garn's west ridge. Follow this path down to Idwal Cottage.

Carnedd y Filiast Expedition
Total climb 300m: Grade 3

At the northern end of the Glyderau range lies Carnedd y Filiast (Cairn of the Greyhound Bitch) whose eastern slopes sweep down into Cwm Graianog. The north side of the cwm is dominated by a vast expanse of

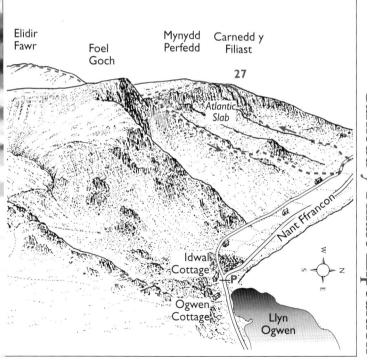

tilted gritstone slabs over 300m high. The slabs are visible – notably from the A5 near Bethesda – but look improbable, seeming too smooth to climb. But climbed they are, if infrequently, by a number of excellent long routes; the best lines often being on the edges of the overlapping slabs.

The most impressive of these slabs is the huge Atlantic Slab with its rippled surface and numerous narrow horizontal bands of quartz. This vast easy-angled slab is tilted to the north, and up its right-hand edge is an excellent and exposed 300m Grade 3 scramble, known as The Ridge and graded in climbing guides as Moderate.

This is a long, serious outing that follows a broken ridge and series of interconnecting slabs, avoiding difficulties as they arrive, usually by traversing into grass and heather grooves on the right. Low down the rock is smooth and can be difficult in wet weather, but higher up the surface becomes rough and much easier to climb. If the edge of the slab is followed on the upper part of the route then this will involve moves on small holds with considerable exposure, and some may prefer to treat it as a roped climb. Small wires in cracks provide good protection. The route cannot be easily reversed or escaped from.

27. Atlantic Slab Grade 3
Vertical height about 300m; Guide time about 3 hours.

Approach: The best approach is directly up the hillside from just south of Tai-newyddion Farm on the old Nant Ffrancon road at a cattle grid (SH632632). There is very limited parking here so you are better parking further south up the road just beyond another cattle grid (SH638623) or in the car parks near Ogwen Cottage and walking along the old road.

Ascend the steep bracken and grass covered slopes to the south of a stream into Cwm Graianog until you meet a wire fence, then follow this up left to the foot of the south-bounding grassy ridge. Cross the fence at a stile and follow the ridge until you are above an old sheepfold in the cwm. From here you can familiarize yourself with the confusing layout of the various slabs on the opposite side of the cwm.

A stone wall runs along the entire base of the slabs and abuts against the overlap below the smooth narrow Russet Slab, high up on the left. To the right of Russet Slab is the vast expanse of the tilted Atlantic Slab, its rippled surface dappled with lines of quartz and grassy runnels. Below

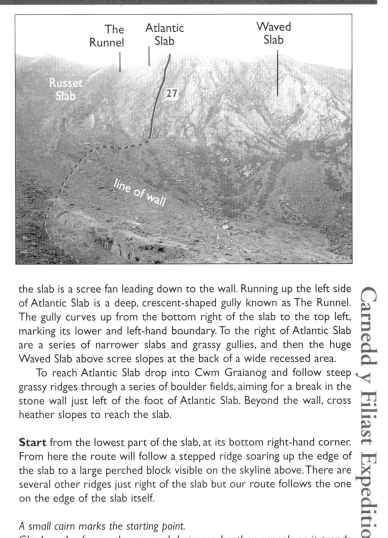

The Runnel

Atlantic Slab

Waved Slab

Russet Slab

27

line of wall

the slab is a scree fan leading down to the wall. Running up the left side of Atlantic Slab is a deep, crescent-shaped gully known as The Runnel. The gully curves up from the bottom right of the slab to the top left, marking its lower and left-hand boundary. To the right of Atlantic Slab are a series of narrower slabs and grassy gullies, and then the huge Waved Slab above scree slopes at the back of a wide recessed area.

To reach Atlantic Slab drop into Cwm Graianog and follow steep grassy ridges through a series of boulder fields, aiming for a break in the stone wall just left of the foot of Atlantic Slab. Beyond the wall, cross heather slopes to reach the slab.

Start from the lowest part of the slab, at its bottom right-hand corner. From here the route will follow a stepped ridge soaring up the edge of the slab to a large perched block visible on the skyline above. There are several other ridges just right of the slab but our route follows the one on the edge of the slab itself.

A small cairn marks the starting point.
Climb a rib of smooth, grey rock between heather runnels as it trends

Carnedd y Filiast Expedition

up slightly left for about 20m to meet the ridge proper. Follow the general line of the ridge, keeping to its crest as much as possible: there is some delightful scrambling with good holds but in places it will be necessary to avoid harder moves by stepping into grooves on the right below the overlap. This will involve swapping good rock for a mixture of perched blocks, heather and bilberry.

A series of short slabs with wide cracks and a few deep clefts are interspersed with pleasant sections of ridge scrambling, often in airy positions with steep drops on the right. Continue up the broken ridge, and short connecting slabs, to eventually arrive at the perched block at half-height.

Above the block climb up the easier angled ridge. When the overlap on the edge of the slab diminishes you can either follow the edge of the main slab itself or the groove to the right. In dry conditions the best line is up a series of faint grassy runnels on the slab just left of its edge. Here good holds on rough gritstone give some easy but exposed scrambling in a superb position with the long sweep of slab below pulling at your ankles. There are good resting ledges and although the slab is easy angled, a rope would be useful on this long section.

When the angle eases at the top of the slab, traverse up left over broken rocks, and then ascend grassy slopes for a short distance to the summit of Carnedd y Filiast. By walking left round the lip of Cwm Graianog you get a tremendous view back across to the top of Atlantic Slab.

And now? You can return to the starting point by descending the south bounding ridge of Cwm Graianog. A finer continuation to the day though is to head south to the summit of Mynydd Perfedd accompanied by fine views to the right of the dammed Marchlyn Mawr backed by the shapely peak of Elidir Fawr.

A great way of extending the expedition is to walk south-west from Mynydd Perfedd down to Bwlch y Marchlyn and ascend a sharp ridge up to the summit of Elidir Fawr. Back at Bwlch y Marchlyn you can contour east across grassy slopes to Bwlch y Brecan between Mynydd Mawr and Foel Goch. Bwlch y Brecan can also be reached directly by a steep descent south-east from Mynydd Mawr.

From the Bwlch y Brecan easy but steep grass slopes lead east back down to the valley bottom and the old Nant Ffrancon road.

Carnedd y Filiast Expedition

Snowdon and Llanberis Pass

No mountaineer ever called it Mount Snowdon. It is just Snowdon, or if you prefer, Yr Wyddfa: the highest peak in Wales and also the finest. Cadair Idris may be more beautiful; Tryfan may be more purely a climber's peak; but Snowdon has it all. The summit cafe is monstrous (there are plans for a new building, which looks as if it should be a great improvement) and the railway an anachronism: if it didn't already exist, there's no way they'd be allowed to build it today. But Snowdon is big enough, and mountain enough, to bear these slights with dignity.

Yr Wyddfa is a complex mountain, or series of mountains: there are six main ridges leading to the summit. Five have walkers' paths on or near them. The sixth, Crib Goch, is a bit more than a walk. And there are

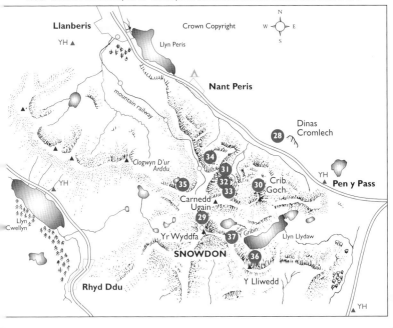

many subsidiary ridges delineating deep cwms, especially on the north side. There is a wealth of possibility here for the climber, the scrambler, and anyone who loves to explore.

The high crags in these cwms are mist-shrouded and forbidding; even in the most benign conditions they demand respect. It's the nature of glaciated landscapes – and Snowdon is the textbook example of a glaciated mountain – that the corries and the grandest crags generally have a northern or eastern aspect. It's quite a bonus, therefore, that low on the southern slopes of the Glyderau, a stone's throw from the road though the Llanberis Pass – simply 'The Pass' to climbers – is a series of steep, south-facing crags.

Being low down and having no pretensions to leading to any summit, they were largely ignored by the early pioneers, only coming into their own under a generation of climbers who had cut their teeth on the gritstone crags of the Peak District. On Tryfan or Lliwedd, many of the great deeds were done a century or more ago. On the Llanberis crags, the Golden Age began after the Second World War and many of the protagonists are still around.

Hard by the road, on the Cromlech Boulders, a distinct sub-culture of climbing exists, where whole days may be spent breathing diesel fumes and grappling with a few metres of rock. It's a far cry from the high ridges and lonely cwms. But it is all climbing. Nowhere in Britain can the full gamut covered by the word be better seen. Yes, Snowdon has it all.

Access

Access centres on the A4086, which runs from Llanberis through the Pass and on to Capel Curig. Car-parking in the Pass and at its summit, Pen y Pass, is usually in short supply. Fortunately, the Snowdon Sherpa bus services are already good and likely to get better; and with Pen y Pass as their link-up point, they provide access to Snowdon from all sides. S1 connects Llanberis and the Park and Ride car-park at Gwastadnant with the climbs in Llanberis Pass and with Pen y Pass. S2 and S3 run from Pen y Pass to Capel Curig then diverge to Betws-y-Coed and Bethesda respectively. The S4 service runs between Beddgelert and Caernarfon. There's also the 97/97A/98 service connecting Porthmadog, Beddgelert and Pen y Pass to Betws-y-Coed.

This liberates the walker and climber from the tyranny of the circular route. To avoid anxiety about catching the last bus, the best plan is usually to start the day with a bus journey and plan the route to finish at your valley base or parked car. For instance, someone staying at Llanberis can catch the first bus at 0830, do any of the routes that start from The Pass or Pen y Pass and then have a choice of routes for a walk back to base. Specific suggestions will be made for some of the routes but there are so many options it's impossible to list them all.

Amenities
Apart from the dubious blessings of the cafe on its summit, Snowdon has plenty of facilities around its flanks. Pride of place, on basis of altitude, goes to the Youth Hostel at Pen y Pass. In its former incarnation as

Looking down the cliffs of Clogwyn D'ur Arddu to its little lake

the Gorphwysfa Hotel it played host to many famous climbers, including George Mallory of Everest. A hundred metres lower and just over a kilometre to the east, the Pen-y-Gwryd hotel was the base for generations of (slightly posher) climbers and, most famously, for much of the training of the 1953 Everest expedition.

Heading down the Pass, there are campsites, bunkhouses and climbing club huts right in the heart of things. There's inexpensive farm camping at Blaen-y-Nant, right at the start of Route 30; and more at Nant Peris. B&B and pub accommodation begins a little lower down at Gwastadnant and Nant Peris, and there's plenty more in and around Llanberis.

For food and drink, there is a cafe at Pen y Pass and the aforementioned Pen-y-Gwryd Hotel. Going down the Pass, the first pub is the tremendously popular Vaynol Arms. In Llanberis the climbers' watering holes have always been the Padarn Lake Hotel and the Victoria, but The Heights, with its ensuite climbing wall, is also now in favour. Pete's Eats is the definitive climbers' cafe. It's one of very few in the world to have a New Climbs book, and it buys over a ton of spuds every week, virtually all destined to be turned into chips; healthier options are also available!

Llanberis has several climbing gear shops, including the original Joe Brown's. There's a second Joe Brown branch at Capel Curig, along with a couple of other outlets.

Valley Crag: Dinas Cromlech

The Cromlech, as it is often called, is by Welsh standards middle-sized or even small. But as you descend the road towards Pont-y-Cromlech, its dominating position and dramatic form – not to mention its history – make it a big crag in everything except that small matter of being under 100m high.

From this angle, and from directly below, the dominant feature of the crag is its central open-book corner. That diedre is Cenotaph Corner, one of the most famous of all British rock climbs. It can be hard to believe that Cenotaph is only a single pitch, less than 40m high. Its first ascent by Joe Brown in 1952 is the stuff of legend. A line which had beaten many of the leading climbers of the day succumbed to a 21-year-old plumber from Manchester, climbing in socks because the route was

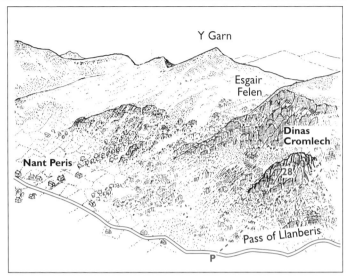

damp. Brown went on to make many notable climbs in the Alps and Himalaya, including the first ascent of Kangchenjunga, the world's 3rd-highest peak, and is still climbing more than 50 years on.

Cenotaph's flanking walls house even harder routes; Left Wall (E3), Right Wall (E5) and Lord of the Flies (E6) are on the hit-list of every climber who can contemplate those grades. Towards its right edge the crag becomes more broken, and in places vegetated. This area, so easily overlooked at first glance, houses what has been voted the best V.Diff in Britain. But is it really better than Amphitheatre Buttress, or for that matter Bowfell Buttress, Bosigran Ridge or Cioch Nose Direct? There's only one way to be sure...

28. Flying Buttress 97m V. Diff
Guide time about 2 hours
Flying Buttress is essential for any V. Diff leader, as Cenotaph Corner is for the E1 climber. The line may appear unlikely to 'go' at such a lowly grade; it is certainly steep, and it serves up buckets of exposure. Whether this is exhilarating or terrifying depends on you, but excellent

Valley Crag: Dinas Cromlech

protection helps and so does an abundance of holds. For this is where all of the jug-handle holds, so noticeably missing from Cenotaph Corner, have ended up.

Approach
One can enthuse indefinitely about the climb, but there's nothing good to be said about the walk up to the crag, which is nasty, brutish, and longer than it should be. 25 minutes is a fair time if you don't want to arrive a physical and mental wreck.

The starting point is an open space just east of the famous Cromlech Boulders (which sometimes, these days, are busier than the main crag). There are lay-bys here but they're often choked. Fortunately there is also a bus stop (Sherpa service S1).

It's worth getting your bearings from here. There'll be no doubt about Cenotaph Corner, but unless the light's just right the semi-detached ridge of Flying Buttress can be a lot less obvious. It rises about 80m right of Cenotaph Corner and a little lower than its foot, above an unmistakable landmark in the form of a long horizontal streak of white quartz.

Approach: Slog up the eroded scree paths. There are many lines, none of them pleasant. Some bluffs around half-height are best taken at their extreme right but even so a little mild scrambling is called for. Above this it doesn't get any better. Most of the paths lead up towards Cenotaph Corner and it's probably best to follow them – you'll want a look anyway – before heading up to the right, along the base of the crag, to the quartz band.

Start: The route starts just to right of the right-hand end of the quartz. From here its lower section – the flying buttress itself – looms above dauntingly, tapering to a pointed crest. It looks a bit steep for a V. Diff.

1. (27m) The first few metres are relatively broken but a steeper wall rears just above. Climb this by a shallow groove to a ledge (possible belay). Continue up another steep wall, aiming for a notch on the skyline, beyond which there's a good ledge. Continue up a short wall to an even better ledge. If for some reason you've thought better of the whole thing, it's possible to escape to the right here – the last escape on the route.

Valley Crag: Dinas Cromlech

Dinas Cromlech

Cenotaph Corner

28

Pinnacles

Flying Buttress

from Pass of Llanberis

2. (18m) Some care is needed to avoid rope-drag on this pitch, as it climbs over a series of pinnacles.

Climb the more broken face above the belay, which still retains some vegetation, to the spiky crest of the buttress. Traverse along the crest, keeping to its right side, and then climb down into the notch at its end: a grassy haven separating the buttress from the main crag. Belay here, and wonder where the hell it goes next.

3. (16m) Take care to protect the second on this pitch.

The main crag looms steeply over the notch. Short walls and ledges form two steps at the base of the steep wall. Climb to the upper ledge then move left to the very edge of the wall, where the exposure really

Valley Crag: Dinas Cromlech

starts to bite. Take a deep breath and move round the edge. Step down and cross a groove, then move left again onto a slab. A line of big flake holds runs up left, to the skyline. Here you find large flake belays but only a tiny stance.

4. (21m) Step off the highest flake onto the wall above. Make a few moves diagonally left to the edge of the wall, then climb up to the start of a slabby gangway that runs up to the right. Don't miss the providential thread runner just above this point. Now follow the gangway to a large ledge at its top. It's palatial after the previous stance, but belays are harder to arrange; climb up a couple of metres to find the best nut crack..

5. (15m) There is just one weakness in the wall above: a right-leaning crack that soon broadens into a chimney. The move to get established in the chimney has a certain notoriety but doesn't have to be that hard. Rather than trying to hide in the chimney as soon as it broadens to body-width, the secret is to stay on the outside, using holds on the right wall, for another move or two (a prehensile scrotum also helps). The rest of the chimney is straightforward and soon leads to boulder belays at the top of the crag.

Descent: You can traverse off right from here; but this is a shortcut. Purists will climb a short wall on the left to the domed summit of the Cromlech. This is a fine viewpoint, and unfrequented as most of those who do the harder climbs descend by abseil. Descend the short back wall of the Cromlech to join the other end of the shortcut traverse at a grassy saddle.

Descend from the saddle's back right corner on an eroded path leading into a narrow gully. As the gully swings to the right and becomes broader, work over to its left side (facing downhill). Care is needed on loose ground and there are a few short rock steps, but even so it's easier than the walk up to the crag was.

There is another classic V. Diff on the crag in the shape of Spiral Stairs, which starts at the base of the left wall of Cenotaph Corner, but a long

opposite page: Bernie Carter on the first pitch of Flying Buttress (Route 28), Dinas Cromlech

Valley Crag: Dinas Cromlech

(and now very polished) traverse on the first pitch makes it difficult to recommend unless both leader and second are fully competent at the grade, and preferably have a bit in hand.

Snowdon Expedition

Rated by many as the finest walk in Wales, the classic Snowdon Horseshoe is, in the context of this book, a spectacular but undemanding scramble, and often sadly overcrowded. The alternative 'Straightened Horseshoe' that follows (Route 30) uses Crib Goch's slightly harder and much quieter other scrambling ridge: its North one. By hustling past the almost-urban scene at Snowdon summit, and carefully keeping off the path from there to Y Lliwedd, you can avoid quite a lot of the crowds while getting all of the Horseshoe atmosphere.

Return from that route is by the Sherpa bus. There are, however, times when the bus doesn't run. In the glorious hour before the dawn; in midwinter's crisp snow and with 100km views. Those, of course, are exactly the times to enjoy the Horseshoe in its classic form.

Scramblers short of time can enjoy a Shorter Horseshoe by descending Y Gribin (Route 37) instead of continuing over Lliwedd.

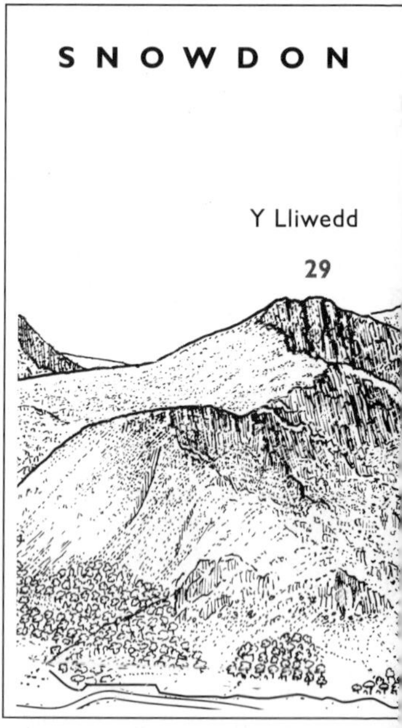

29. Snowdon Horseshoe Grade 1

0.5km of easy scrambling (more if all the scrambling opportunities are taken)
guide time: 5 to 6 hours

From Pen y Pass (SH647556) head out the top of the right-hand car park, signed Pig Track, and follow this up into Bwlch y Moch, the distinctive notch in the hillside that offers fine

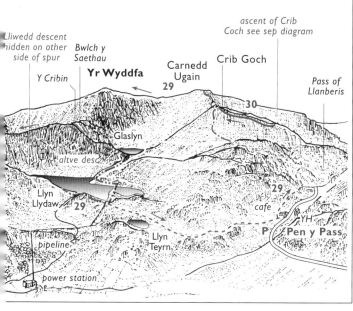

views down over Llyn Llydaw. Bear right here and follow the clear path easily up to right, to reach the foot of the blunt nose of Crib Goch. Now make a direct assault on this face; there are many lines so you can make it as easy or as tough as you desire. The angle eases to easy scrambling on to the preliminary eastern summit.

Follow the knife-edge ridge on to the main summit and down towards Bwlch Goch. This section can be taken on the clean rocks of the crest or by a gritty path down left. The two large pinnacles that end the rock ridge, just before Bwlch Goch, can be turned on the left or climbed over.

Cross the short stretch of grassy ridge across Bwlch Goch onto the rising rock ridge of Crib y Ddysgl. There's plenty of scrambling to the right of the path. Continue over the 1,065m summit of Carnedd Ugain, and keep ahead to join the main Llanberis Path and railway line on the final pull to Snowdon's summit.

The usual Horseshoe path from Snowdon's summit follows the south-west ridge down for 200m to a tall standing stone on the left; then turns sharply left to slant down a rugged stony path into Bwlch y Saethau. Those who actually enjoy scrambling (many poor souls on Crib Goch obviously do not) will take instead the direct East Ridge. The small path zig-zags down scree to the top of a sudden steepening. The rock outcrops below give some down-scrambling on clean well-used rock down to Bwlch y Saethau. (Non-scramblers who avoid the outcrops will find themselves on unpleasant unstable scree lying over bare rock).

As you cross Bwlch y Saethau, there's a scramblers' shortening of the route by descending Y Gribin into Cwm Llydaw on the left – see Route 37.

There's also a good path just down on the right. Ignoring both of these, head up Y Lliwedd keeping as close as possible to the top rim of its fine northern crags for some pleasant scrambling. (For those crags see Route 36.)

A cairn marks the higher west summit of Y Lliwedd, with a nice ridge path round to the 893m east top. The path carries on down the ridge bounding Cwm Llydaw, and then on the right-hand (southern) flank, to a flat boggy shoulder.

A cairn marks the point on the left to drop off onto the face above Llyn Llydaw: this descent is on a steep zig-zag path of scree on bare rock. At the corner of Llyn Llydaw turn right along the smooth Miners' Track which leads easily after 2km to Pen y Pass.

Snowdon Expedition

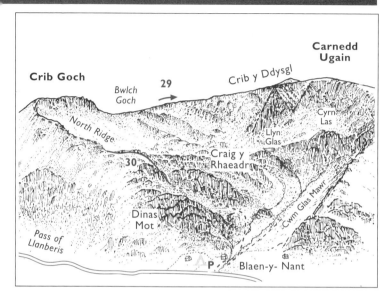

30. The Straightened Horseshoe: North Ridge of Crib Goch Grade 1

Vertical height about 450m, but this includes much walking: guide time about 1 1/2 hours to Crib Goch summit

Beginning the Horseshoe via the North Ridge of Crib Goch instead of the customary East Ridge has several advantages, and this variation, which has rather more scrambling than the regular North Ridge route, has even more. Even before the scrambling starts, it scores points. Instead of the broad, over-engineered and crowded path there's steep grass and boulders from the off. There's time, and peace, to settle into an appreciation of the scale and grandeur of the surroundings, where wild goats still haunt the lonely recesses. The way passes under a dramatic, dripping crag before the scrambling begins in a hidden gully past waterfalls, continuing up a series of inviting rock ribs. The Main Horseshoe route, with its inevitable crowds, is not met until the crest of Crib Goch, which is the bit no-one wants to miss.

Snowdon Expedition

On Crib Goch's North Ridge

Snowdon Expedition

Approach: From the car park and campsite at Blaen-y-nant (SH622569), cross the ladder stile on the right and walk over a rickety bridge. Follow a path up into the cwm (directly uphill) with the stream on your left, to a stile and gap in a wall. About 150m above this, look for a narrow path going off left. The path doesn't last, so aim for an isolated tree and continue in the same general direction, leftwards and slightly uphill above a wall and stream, with minor detours round bogs. The steep wall of Craig y Rhaeadr looms ahead, its central area black and normally wet: the name means Waterfall Crag. It is rarely climbed on in summer, but in a hard winter some of the best ice routes in Wales form here.

About 50m left of the crag a small stream emerges from a rocky hollow in a series of small waterfalls. The scramble starts to right of this stream, crosses it about two-thirds way up the wall of the hollow, and then takes a wandering line up less steep ground, though with plenty of outcrops to maintain interest.

Pass below the wall of Craig y Rhaeadr and aim for the first stream coming down left of the crag, in a little gill or gully; its foot is at SH622561. About half an hour to here.

Start where the channel becomes rocky. Climb an easy grey rock rib immediately right of the stream. Where the rock steepens sharply after a few metres, a direct ascent is possible but more like Grade 2. A subsidiary slot about 7m right offers the easier option.

Keep on up rock and heather to the right of the stream; traces of a path appear. Continue until just above the largest waterfall, which can be heard but is not easily seen. Here there's a heathery shelf with the remains of a small cairn. Walk left along the shelf to overlook the stream and continue round to follow a small ledge on the side wall. Where this ends, step down to beside a small pool between cascades. Cross the stream to an eroded path on the other side.

Go up this for 20m to a narrow easy-angled rib of grey rock which rises from right beside the path. Follow this rib pleasantly until it broadens out. Work across the left flank of the rib into a small heather bay, and back out to the right onto the continuation of the grey rib. Climb a steep little step and then more broken ground to a broad shelf with patches of scree.

A square slabby buttress above has a steep start. It's easier to go up

Snowdon Expedition

the flaky wall a few metres to its left . After 10m this peters out; move right, onto the upper reaches of the buttress. From its top bear left to a continuous but easy-angled rib, and carry on up by ad hoc scrambling and then walking, to reach a minor top on the crest of the broad ridge above Dinas Mot.

Walk to the right (south) straight up the ridge, wide and easy at first, until it steepens again, rising as a cone covered in reddish scree. Well-worn paths weave across and up the slope, until more solid rock takes over higher up. From the apex of the cone a narrow, spiky ridge connects to the summit of Crib Goch, where the classic Horseshoe route is met.

Continue on Route 29 (above), taking care to avoid the main path as suggested wherever possible.

Carnedd Ugain Expedition
200m scrambling, 75m climbing at up to Diff

Garnedd Ugain (or Crib y Ddysgl as it's often known) has the honour of being England and Wales's 2nd highest peak, and a fine mountain it is too, especially when approached from the delightful Cwm Glas. For the record, Carnedd Ugain is the true name of the 1065m summit; the Ordnance Survey misspells it as Garnedd; and Crib y Ddysgl is the narrow ridge that's slung between this summit and Bwlch Goch. Nevertheless, the summit is still regularly referred to as Crib y Ddysgl. The itinerary described here makes a fine full-day expedition that tracks all the way from the floor of the Llanberis Pass, via some remote walking, some varied scrambling, and an absolutely top quality rock climb that surprisingly goes at just Diff. Further scrambling moves lead to Carnedd Ugain's summit; where Crib Goch's North Ridge or the seldom trod Cwm Glas ridge lead back down to the Pass.

31. Cyrn Las Grade 3
Vertical Height 150m; Guide time 45 minutes

The broken crags of Cyrn Las have little to offer the scrambler or lower-grade climber, but the rocky shoulder that bounds the towering black buttress to the left offers some wonderful sport; clean rock

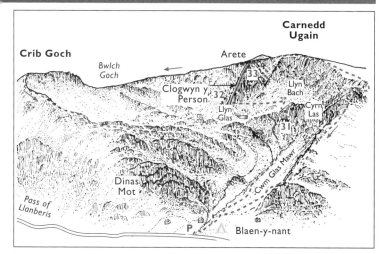

follows a cascading stream from the floor of Cwm Glas Mawr right up to the rim of the upper cwm.

The opening few moves are the trickiest; the rock is slabby and holds are thin on the ground when you need them most. It's worth keeping the rope handy, maybe even moving together, although protection is pretty thin on this section too. After this, it's straightforward Grade One fun that's considerably more enjoyable than the footpath that travels the same way. The scrambling also acts as a great warm-up for the Parson's Nose.

Approach: From the car park and campsite at Blaen-y-nant (SH622569), cross the ladder stile on the right and walk over a rickety bridge. Follow a path up into the cwm (directly uphill) with the stream on your left. Go through a gap in a wall and continue until the gradient eases at around 400m altitude. You can now see the true lie of the land, with the towering crags of Cyrn Las directly ahead. The scramble ahead will be aiming for the high shoulder to the left of these. Continue with stream on your left until the rocky wall that forms the left-hand foot of Cyrn Las blocks your path. Follow a scree path up to its foot.

Start approximately 5m to the right of the stream on an easy-angled

Carnedd Ugain Expedition

Carnedd Ugain Expedition

skirt of rock.

Head upwards keeping the stream close to your left. After a couple of difficult moves on slabby rock, the gradient eases.

The remainder of the scramble is typical Grade 1, whereby part of the fun lies in chosing your own line. Either climb the small craggy faces or, if you'd prefer, move around them. After a vertical 100m of broken scambling, you'll come to a fairly large grassy terrace.

To your right, a continuation of this terrace breaks the left-hand edge of Cyrn Las into two. You need to keep straight up however, keeping these crags of Cyrn Las to your right and continuing over over short crags and grassy terraces to the lip of Cwm Glas.

Next: Keep to the right, passing just above a wonderful waterfall on the lip of the cwm, and then walk over to Llyn Bach. Above you, forming the left hand wall of the cwm, is the steely-grey crag of Clogwyn y Person. This tapers into a sharp arete – the Clogwyn y Person Arete – that defines its left-hand side. The foot of this arete consists of a steep nose of dark rock: this is the Parson's Nose. It's split from the main crag by the deeply cloven Western Gully; which is the line of a scramble (Grade 2) that could be used to reach the scrambling on the Clogwyn y Person Arete without the climb on the Parson's Nose.

Make your way around the lake and clamber up to the foot of the arete.

32. The Parson's Nose 75m Diff
Guide time 1 1/2 hours

This is a wonderfully atmospheric climb that leads neatly onto a fine scramble and eventually up to a noteworthy top. The climb itself only goes as far as the top of the Western Gully but there's still plenty of rock beyond here, with another climbing pitch required to gain the Clogwyn y Person Arete and possibly another one after that, although a competent party might choose to move together for these sections. The positions are as grand as anything in this book, yet the difficulties are few, making it one of Snowdonia's finest outings at the grade. Unbelievably, the first ascent was in 1884, credited to an A. H. Stocker.

Start at the very lowest point of the nose.

Carnedd Ugain Expedition

1. (25m) This pitch is little more than a scramble. Climb the slabby nose, keeping as close to the actual crest as possible. Continue over a few ledges until you reach the foot of a much steeper face. Belay a few metres to the right of the crest, where there are some nut placements.

2. (25m) Traverse back left to the crest at the foot of a steep wall. A groove up the centre of this wall holds a vertical crack: the way up this crack is marked by well-polished footholds.

After 10m move right, away from the groove, and then trend up and rightwards on knobbly holds that lead to a good ledge, beneath a steeper wall, where you can belay.

3. (25m) Climb the wall above the belay and keep trending rightwards until you reach an exposed arete with the Western Gully to your right. Continue easily up the arete until its angle eases at the top of the nose, with the deep cleft, that seperates you from the main arete, straight ahead. Belay from here.

33. Clogwyn y Person Arete Grade 3
Vertical Height 150m; Guide time 45 minutes

Climb down into the deep cleft that splits the stance from the main arete. Move left for a couple of metres to locate a polished groove that runs up onto the main face. Climb up this groove to a terrace, where you'll meet a path (this is the top of the Western Gully scramble). Don't follow the path but instead turn left to climb an easy but steep wall, about 5m high, and continue upwards towards the crest. You'll soon reach a huge quartzy ledge backed up by a steep wall that's split by a large crack. Climb this wall to reach another ledge that marks the top of this section.

From here, it's a case of scrambling up to the crest of the ridge and then following this as it gets easier and easier. Eventually it becomes a footpath with further scrambling opportunities to the right. Follow the arete up to the summit trig point of Carnedd Ugain.

And now? From here you have two choices. A left turn over Crib Goch and down its North Ridge (reversing Route 30) offers plenty more scrambling and will be most most appealing if the hour is late and the crowds have vanished from Crib Goch. The alternative is the Cwm Glas Ridge, the narrow rocky spur that splits the two valleys of Cwm Glas Mawr and Cwm Glas Bach. It's more of a walk than a scramble but it's very direct and offers some great views as well as plenty of solitude. Probably the best option on a busy weekend.

Descent by Crib Goch's North Ridge

Trace the ridge of Crib y Ddysgl, with plenty more scrambling on offer, down into Bwlch Goch.

Clogwyn y Person from Llyn Glas

You can then scramble on along the famous Pinnacle Ridge onto Crib Goch itself.

From the futhest (easternmost) summit of Crib Goch, turn north onto the fine but slightly crumbly arete. It starts quite steeply but soon levels to make easy walking. At the arete's end, descend the scree cone on zigzag paths to the top of the grassy lower ridge. Continuing northwards would lead to the top of Dinas Mot crags, so care is now needed. Head down northwest, passing through a couple of quartz bands, to find a small stream in a grassy hollow among outcrops. The grid ref here is SH 6223 5602. Head down to right of this stream: as the ground

Carnedd Ugain Expedition

steepens the stream forms a little rocky gill, with a zig-zag path involving a little scrambling to its right.

The stream splashes down into a side-hollow of Cwm Glas Mawr, which is followed down to Blaen-y-nant.

Descent by the Cwm Glas Ridge

Bear right at Carnedd Ugain's trig point and follow the escarpment edge around to the north for 500m, where you can drop down onto a prominent grassy nose that leads down onto the Cwm Glas Ridge. Continue northwards down the ever-narrowing ridge, with a few scrambly moves, until this peters out in the confines of Cwm Glas Mawr, close to the wall that you passed through on the way up. Bear right to the stream and then bear left to follow it back down to the car park.

Clogwyn Du'r Arddu Expedition
300m scrambling, up to Grade 2

Clogwyn Du'r Arddu is invariably shortened to 'Cloggy', and not just by

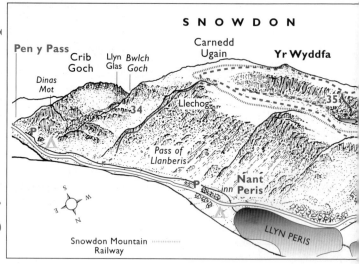

Saesneg (English) climbers who can't get their tongues round the language. Whatever you call it, it is a magnificent crag and has been Mecca to several generations of climbers. Though there is little climbing below VS standard, there are a couple of routes for scramblers. The ascent of the Eastern Terrace, in particular, allows full appreciation of the most handsome crag in Britain.

The usual walk-in from Llanberis is everything the crag is not – easy and rather boring – hence the suggested approach by Llechog. This is unconventional but infinitely more fitting, and the combination makes for a rugged and intriguing mountain day.

34. Llechog West Rib Grade 2
Vertical height about 400 metres in total, but about 200m of actual scrambling: guide time about 1 1/2 hours

There's more than one Llechog on the flanks of Snowdon. This is the one that looms above Gwastadnant, where the crags begin to close in on the way up the Pass. The main buttress looks steep and forbidding but can be scrambled at Grade 3. Our route is easier but longer: not a majestic line

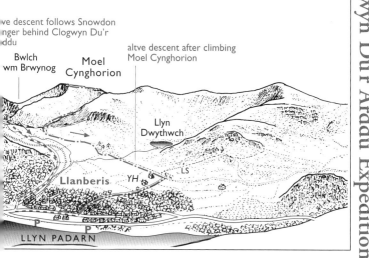

ve descent follows Snowdon
nger behind Clogwyn Du'r
ddu

altve descent after climbing
Moel Cynghorion

Bwlch
wm Brwynog

Moel
Cynghorion

Llyn
Dwythwch

LS

Llanberis   YH

P   P

LLYN PADARN

Clogwyn Du'r Arddu Expedition

but good in detail, with some excellent rock, and worthwhile in its own right even if you don't continue to Cloggy.

As described, it is a pleasant Grade 2, and a very good way of gaining height. It is open to much variation. Easier options, generally on the left, can involve little more than steep walking; harder variations, some of them much harder, are also available. There are traces of a path alongside, but no obvious evidence of previous traffic on the described line.

Approach: The day's route is a horseshoe, not a circle, and the best plan is to park at Llanberis and catch a bus (Sherpa S1) at the outset, rather than at the end, of the day. Alight at Cae Perthi (SH615576). If you insist on coming by car, the nearest parking is at the Gwastadnant Park and Ride or the lay-bys below Clogwyn y Grochan.

From the bus stop (and letter box), walk about 50m in the Llanberis direction. A track goes down to a bridge over the river. Follow the track up and through a wall gap 20m to right of the highest cottage. The main Llechog Buttress looms on the skyline, steep and intimidating: our route will take the easier rocks to its right. Cross a wet patch and walk straight up the hillside towards the first easy-angled rock rib.

Start at the base of this rib. The amount of true scrambling you'll get on this opening section depends on your ability, your determination, and the time you're prepared to spend. The first rock-steps have steep lower faces; most people will circumvent these initial rocks on one side or the other. Walk up to a much longer and broader rib; this rib lies about half way up the slope below the main buttress.

The overall angle of this rib is low but there are some steep steps on quite smooth rock, while the line of grassy weaknesses weaving up the centre of the rib is not quite the soft option it may appear; there are a couple of awkward greasy steps.

The top of the rib is a distinct grassy shelf. The main Llechog buttress glowers above, still some distance higher with a plinth of more broken rock. Over to the right now is the start of the West Rib, with a steep little buttress forming its foot. Above this little buttress is an obvious notch and just a little higher again, a saddle crossed by a stone wall. Walk across almost horizontally to this saddle.

A wire fence continues the line of the wall. Climb up steeply just left of this to get onto the next rib just above its base. The rib is quite steep

Clogwyn Du'r Arddu Expedition

Lechog Rib

34

at first but the angle soon eases. Carry on over grass and boulders to the base of the next steeper step. A direct ascent of the nose looks attractive but only if you climb about HVS. The first obvious weakness to the left is a gully/groove, splashed with quartz and not very inviting: nor is the chimney just left again. Instead walk up still further left to a spike on the skyline.

About 10m above and slightly to the right is a prominent perched block. To reach it, move up and right to a narrow rock ledge, then up again to a grass ledge. A few metres right, climb a heathery weakness to the perched block, now seen to be one of several. Climb up behind the big block on the right; step from this onto heathery slabs and then up easily to a large grass terrace.

From the right end of the grass terrace climb a short, low-angled rib and over a pile of blocks. The next step is topped by a projecting block: climb up slightly to the right of this. Climb over more blocks and then up bubbly rock on the left flank of the next clean rib to gain its top.

Clogwyn Du'r Arddu

Climb the next step by diagonal twin cracks and then go up a low-angled rib to right of a heathery weakness, to below another pile of blocks. Clamber through and over the blocks and climb the thin flake above to gain easier ground.

The next rib, just above and right, has a steep lower nose hanging over space. It's possible to climb a short wide crack just above the nose to reach some blocks in a spectacular position. If this looks too alarming, the rib crest can also be gained higher up. Now follow this crest until it levels out.

There's now a distinct break and above it the rock changes character, being more spiky in appearance, especially on the left. Traces of a path are visible, flirting with the prickly crest, but the prickles can be taken directly. It's never very difficult but the rock is more brittle than that below. A final steepening can be avoided on the left or climbed, over splintered rock, on the right. Above is a level shoulder on the main ridge dividing Llanberis Pass from Cwm Brwynog.

Next: You can, of course, return to Llanberis very easily from here. Sliding down the cog-rail on slabs of slate, as Joe Brown and co. used to do after days climbing on Cloggy, is definitely not recommended! But Cloggy is now seen directly ahead and at roughly the same level. The remaining hazards are a barbed wire fence (stile a short way left) and then the crossing of the railway track.

Walk across the open moor: a level course aims a little left of Cloggy. If you stick to the 650m contour you will cross the broad Llanberis track shortly before meeting the narrower climbers' path which swings round the back of the cwm, below the broken sprawl of Clogwyn Coch, to Cloggy. The complex structure of the crag gradually becomes clearer, resolving into distinct crags or buttresses. The two terraces form a broad open 'V'. The principal climbing areas are the East Buttress, below the left (Eastern) Terrace, and the West Buttress, which rises above the Western Terrace.

35. Eastern Terrace Grade 1

Vertical height about 100m: guide time about 30 minutes.

Standing near the dark waters of Llyn Du'r Arddu, which lies in a hollow at the

Clogwyn Du'r Arddu

West Buttress

The Pinnacle

Great Slab

The Boulder

Eastern Terrace

Western Terrace

35

Great Wall

East Buttress

Llyn Du'r Arddu

foot of the buttresses, few can fail to feel a sense of awe at the magnificent architecture of the crag. It is a place redolent with the history of Welsh rock climbing.
Numerous classic routes weave their way up the vertical walls and cracks of the
East Buttress, and the overlapping and steep-angled slabs of West Buttress. For
scramblers there is just one feasible route, the Eastern Terrace (Grade 1). The
Western Terrace used to be a popular scramble until the late 1980s when a section of the slabs overhanging the terrace collapsed. Due to the large amount of
rock debris on the terrace this route is not recommended.

The Eastern Terrace route, first ascended in 1798 by the Reverends Bingley and
Williams when seeking out plant specimens, traverses to the right below the East
Buttress then turns left up the widening terrace as it slants across a huge cliff. Today
it's used as a descent route for climbers and can be busy on summer weekends.
The scrambling, though easy, is interesting and the rock scenery throughout is
tremendous.

Clogwyn Du'r Arddu

Start at the foot of the impressive East Buttress with its plethora of hard, classic routes such as Vember, Indian Face and Master's Wall.

Scramble to the right along the foot of East Buttress up a slanting line following well-marked quartz ledges, followed by some steeper steps leading towards a deep gully. Pass below the foot of the gully and traverse right to easier ground, partly overhung by the steep buttress known as The Boulder – some boulder! Here the boulder-strewn Eastern Terrace runs back up to the left.

Scramble up the right-hand (inner) side of the Terrace by a series of damp steps close under overhangs, with good holds overcoming any difficulties. Trend left up an easy polished grove to reach easier angled terrain. Ahead is a huge slab of rock where a zigzagging line is followed up a series of little ledges. After about 30m you meet more open and rubble-strewn ledges. Follow a scree runnel, taking care not to dislodge any rocks onto climbers on the buttresses below the terrace. The scree runs into grassy slopes above the buttresses. Keep uphill, where the Snowdon Ranger Path is soon reached.

And now? Several options present themselves. The keen will follow the path up to the summit of Yr Wyddfa (Snowdon), about 200m higher and a little over a kilometre away.

A more attractive, and certainly quieter, option is to follow the Snowdon Ranger Path down to the west as far as Bwlch Cwm Brwynog. For maximum brownie points ascend Moel Cynghorion – a fine viewpoint in evening light – and descend on the same heading to meet a footpath at Helfa-fain (SH583575); this can be followed down to Llanberis.

More easily, drop down right from the bwlch into Cwm Brwynog. Descend this, keeping to the east (right) of the stream, where a climbers' path to/from Cloggy can be found. This leads to Hafodty Newydd (SH588577) from where a lane takes you down into Llanberis.

Lliwedd Expedition

Lliwedd is the biggest cliff in Wales or England. Combine this fact with a pleasant approach (much pleasanter than that to Dinas Cromlech, for instance), and you may wonder why it is not more popular. But Lliwedd

Clogwyn Du'r Arddu Expedition

Y Lliwedd

is not to modern tastes. Even the easiest routes are serious and committing. The crag is notorious for sloping holds, widely-spaced protection and barely adequate belays. It is also an easy crag to get lost on! Climbing on Lliwedd is a serious business; in its all-round demands it is a step or two up even from Tryfan East Face or Glyder Fach.

If that all sounds off-putting, think again. With greater challenges come greater rewards. A competent party, in good conditions, will have one of the finest mountain days in Britain.

36. Slanting Buttress Ridge Route 229m V. Diff
Guide time about 5 hours

Slanting Buttress lies near the right edge of the crag, and isn't quite as long as the routes on the two main buttresses, making it a good introduction to climbing on Lliwedd. Even so it is still the second longest route in this book. A relatively easy start gets you swiftly to the meat of the route, high above the screes, lost in shadows while Llyn Llydaw glows blue in the sunshine far below.

Descriptions in other guidebooks that suggest a continuous ladder of jugs are misleading as there are several short sections where the Lliwedd recipe of sloping holds can be savoured. The rock is quite clean

Lliwedd Expedition

Lliwedd Expedition

Peter Rawson on Pitch 7, Slanting Buttress

for a high, north-facing crag, but it is still a hostile place in wet conditions. First climbed in 1904.

Approach is invariably made, in about an hour, from Pen y Pass. Car-parking here is expensive and space is limited (suggesting, by the law of supply and demand, that it isn't expensive enough!); good reasons to use the excellent Sherpa bus services. Another is the smugness you will feel as you pass misguided walkers making the unpleasant climb by road from Pen-y-Gwryd. An early start is advisable, whether to catch a parking space, or to ensure you don't miss the last bus; and, indeed, to tackle the climb without background worries about benightment.

From the back left corner of the car-park, follow the broad, easy Miners' Track, past little Llyn Teyrn, to the shores of Llyn Llydaw. Now branch off left on a well-trodden track. After a few hundred metres cross Llydaw's outlet stream (Afon Glaslyn) and then begin to climb. Near the top of the first rise, a narrow and roughly level path breaks away to the right, contouring round above the lake before slanting up the screes below the crag.

From the approach, the skyline of Lliwedd shows three peaks: West, East and Far East. The biggest routes are on the East and West Buttresses, below their respective peaks. Slanting Buttress lies further right, marked by two huge wavy streaks of quartz at its base. From the foot of the West Buttress follow a small path, above some broken rocks, to the base of the quartz bands.

The lower third of the buttress is a sprawling mass where several lines are possible. Above this, the rock gets decidedly steeper. The key is to identify the point at which this steeper band is to be tackled. Fortunately this is unmistakable. There is a very distinct, often gloomy-looking, recess at the left side of the buttress at about one-third height. Two distinct grooves cut into it, the right v-shaped, the left (which will be the line of our route) more square cut.

Start: At the foot of the right-hand, slightly lower quartz band.

1-3. (100m) Either climb fairly directly to the gloomy recess, or begin by following the lower quartz streak up and right. The climbing up the quartz is easy but there are many loose blocks and few belays. This indirect line also gives more scope for second thoughts.

Where the quartz peters out, traverse almost horizontally left across the lower reaches of a big vegetated bay and then climb directly up into the recess. Belay at the base of the left-hand groove.

4. (16m) Climb the left wall of the groove on good holds, and exit through a cut-out to a ledge. Climb over big flakes on the left to a horizontal bit of ridge where some quartzy blocks provide a choice of belay. Directly above are some ominous overhangs.

5. (12m) Move 2m left then climb a steep little chimney that sneaks past the overhangs. Above is a groove with a narrow slabby rib on its left. Whatever combination of the two you opt for, it's a delicate bit. Belay on a small ledge just above the groove.

6. (9m) Above is a V-groove, polished and tricky. This is technically the hardest bit of the route. In desperate straits, it can be avoided on the left by a vegetated groove and series of ledges. Belay directly above the top of the V-groove on another small ledge.

7. (26m) Move up a couple of metres then work right, onto an exposed arete. This arete is not too difficult, though care is needed with some loose rock. The arete becomes a horizontal crest (a cheval technique optional) which leads to a ledge below a broad wall.

8. (22m) Traverse horizontally right through lush vegetation for about 8m then move up to a recessed ledge. Climb a shallow groove above for 5m, then work out right and up a steep quartzy wall – exposed but straightforward – to a ledge at the base of a big open groove.

9. (12m) A subsidiary rib partly blocks the groove at mid-height, forming a small chimney to its left. Start up the left wall of the groove then step across right, into the chimney. Just above a little chockstone, holds on the rib on the right come into play. After a couple more moves swing out right, onto the rib. Climb it and the little groove to its right, until it is possible to step right again to welcoming ledges. If it's still daylight, you can now begin to relax a little.

10. (32m) Climb up easy-angled slabby rocks, trending generally

Lliwedd Expedition

Far East Buttress
East Buttress
West Buttress
Slanting Buttress
36
Llyn Llydaw

leftwards. A kind of trench provides a route through steeper rock above. More broken but still fairly steep rock now leads out to the summit ridge, within sptting distance of the main ridge path, well-trodden by Snowdon Horseshoe pilgrims.

Next: The obvious route is to follow the ridge path over the twin summits of Lliwedd and on down to Llyn Llydaw, there rejoining the Miners' Track back to Pen y Pass.

Alternatively you can avoid the extra ascent and the eroded descent, and enjoy some pleasant down-scrambling on Y Gribin. After visiting Lliwedd's summit anyway (for after such a climb, no lesser sandwich-sunset spot will do), return past the climb top and head down the northeast ridge towards Bwlch y Saethau. There's a path slightly down left, or

Lliwedd Expedition

scrambling along the brink of the Lliwedd Buttress you just climbed up.

Bwlch y Saethau is the pass of the arrows, referring to a mythic battle involving King Arthur. It's a long narrow col: the spur ahead would offer a scrappy scrambling ascent of Snowdon, supposing there were time for such a diversion.

37.Y Gribin (descent) Grade 1
Vertical height lost 150m: approx time ¹/2 hr

Only Grade 1, and not at the top of its grade at that, the Snowdon Gribin is still a serious scramble, with route to be found and no escapes. While not so magnificent as Crib Goch opposite, it's 99 per cent quieter, well-situated at the focus of rocky slopes, and a whole lot nicer than any of Snowdon's main paths.

This Gribin should not be confused with the 'Glyder Gribin' above Ogwen Cottage. The Glyder Gribin is equally nice, but quite a bit easier.

Lliwedd Expedition

Approach (from Y Lliwedd): Follow the ridge crest through Bwlch y Saethau, ignoring the path running just down on the left (Cwm Llan) side. Before the lowest point of the ridge, cairns running down to the right lead to the top of the Gribin spur. If you miss these, then from a small pool at the col's lowest point a small path turns sharply back right and slants down to the same point.

Start: A little rocky turret marks the top of the spur. Head down the crest for the first steep section and the gentler one below. As the spur steepens again, excursions slightly on the right (Lliwedd) side of the crest may be easier. Continue down the crest line to the less steep slab-by bottom section. Here grooves to left (Glaslyn side) of the crest are the easiest way.

A level grass ridge runs out from the spur foot. Off the tip of this there's a little outcrop scrambling to reach the outflow of Glaslyn, with the wide Miners' Track just beyond.

Scrambling on Y Gribin

Lliwedd Expedition

Bernie Carter on the North Ridge of Crib Goch (Route 30): Craig y Rhaeadr below

Nantlle and Moelwynion

This section covers two distinct areas which lie in the slightly lower hills just south of the main Snowdon massif. The sharp-ridged, grassy Nantlle hills are often overlooked, both literally and figuratively, but it is a mistake to dismiss them out of hand and both the routes described here are well worth doing, with the added attraction that overcrowding is rare.

The quarries around Nantlle are conspicuous in the view from Mynydd Mawr or Craig Cwm Silyn, but they're mere rabbit scrapes compared to those around Blaenau Ffestiniog. Yet the Moelwyn hills, rising above this shattered, eviscerated landscape, remain popular with both walkers and climbers. The climbing is accessible and entertaining and for many this more than makes up for the industrial surroundings.

Although close together as the crow flies, travelling between them is awkward and roundabout so access and amenity details are given separately for each.

Nantlle

The small hills of the Nantlle area (sometimes called the Eifionydd) lie to the south-west of the Snowdon range with the main group being situated to the south of the B4418 road linking Rhyd Ddu, Nantlle and Penygroes, and west of the A4085 Rhyd Ddu to Beddgelert road. Mynydd Mawr, often called the 'elephant mountain' because of its shape when seen from the southern slopes of Snowdon, lies just north of the Rhyd Ddu to Nantlle road.

Due to the generally loose and vegetated nature of the rock in this area there are few routes for scramblers, apart from the excellent Sentries' Ridge on Craig y Bera on the south-east face of Mynydd Mawr. Rock climbers are better catered for with some great routes in Cwm Silyn at the northern end of the Nantlle Ridge, overlooking Cwm Pennant. Here are found the steep buttresses of Craig yr Ogof and the impeccable sweep of the Great Slab.

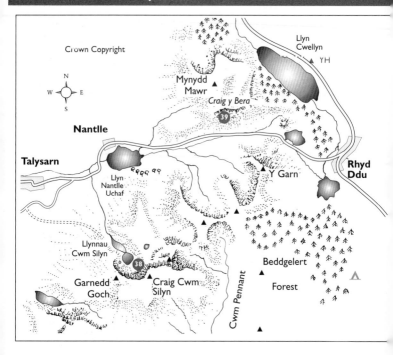

Access

For the car user access is fairly easy, and you can even drive close to Cwm Silyn. There are bus services from Caernarfon and Porthmadog for Penygroes, Rhyd Ddu and Beddgelert. The S4 Snowdon Sherpa bus from Caernarfon passes through Rhyd Ddu and Beddgelert. Also the narrow-gauge Welsh Highland Railway now links Caernarfon with a new station at Rhyd Ddu.

Amenities

The two main centres for exploring the Nantlle area are Rhyd Ddu and Beddgelert. There are B&Bs and hotels in Beddgelert and a popular Forestry Commission campsite just north of the village. There are also various pubs and cafes in Beddgelert.

Accommodation at Rhyd Ddu is limited to a few B&Bs including the

Cwellyn Arms, which also provides bunkhouse accommodation and camping. It provides excellent meals and drinks and was recently voted by CAMRA the best real ale pub in Snowdonia. Just north of Rhyd Ddu is the Snowdon Ranger Youth Hostel.

Rhyd Ddu can also be used as a base for the Snowdon routes, by taking a morning bus to Pen y Pass and finishing the day with an evening walk back down the Snowdon Ranger Path.

Cwm Silyn Expedition

Craig yr Ogof provides the most westerly of the climbs in this book and, with fine views over the coast and the piercing cries of gulls complementing the more commonly heard 'gronk' of the ravens, the climbing on this lonely outpost has a distinctive sea cliff feel to it. The crag consists of two separate faces; one that faces north and the other, the Great Slab, which presides over the steep ground to the south-west. It's this

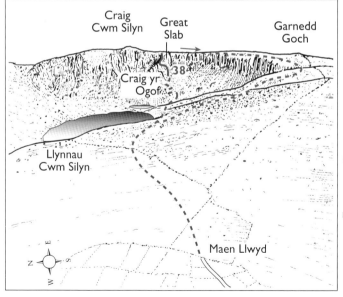

Cwm Silyn Expedition

one we're interested in: in particular the arete that bounds its left-hand side, which carries the classic V. Diff of the crag.

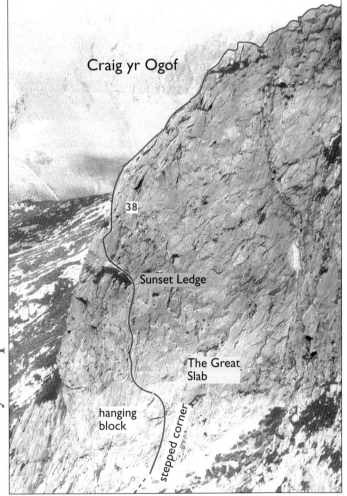

Craig yr Ogof

38

Sunset Ledge

The Great Slab

hanging block

stepped corner

Cwm Silyn Expedition

38. Outside Edge Route 120m V. Diff
Guide time 3 hours

Outside Edge is an atmospheric climb that starts in the middle of the slabby face and trends leftwards to gain its outside edge in some wonderfully exposed positions high above Cwm Silyn's glistening lakes. It's not hard for its grade but some sections are fairly sustained, calling for a dogged and determined approach. Although the route is a single climb, rather than a series of linked routes like most of the outings in this book, it still has the feel of a big mountain expedition to it; particularly the pinnacled upper section, which is quite Alpine in nature. First climbed in 1931.

Approach: Park beyond the gate at the head of the narrow dead-end lane that heads east from Llanllyfni (SH495510). Walk up the well-surfaced track for just over one kilometre and then, as the track starts to drop to the outflow of Llynau Cwm Silyn, hop over a rusty gate on your right. Now follow a path around the hillside, above the lake, eventually dropping to the lake's southern tip. Above you now is a steep scree slope crowned with the impressive faces of Craig yr Ogof. Follow one of the many paths steeply up the scree and head towards the centre of the slabby, south-west facing face.

This face is punctuated at ground level by a stepped corner. To the left of this is a slabby wall with broken holds; 10m above this, you'll see a slender hanging block.

Start 2m to the left of the stepped corner, beneath the hanging block.

1. (15m) Climb straight upwards, over chunky rock with no obvious features, until after a few metres, you arrive on a rightward trending ramp. Follow this for 2m and then climb directly up a steep chimney that leads to the right-hand edge of the hanging block. The top of the block has minimal protection, so trend rightwards to a belay ledge to right of the block.

2. (25m) Move onto the block and then climb awkwardly up the wall above it onto a big ledge 2m higher up. Move to the left hand end of this and then make an exposed rising traverse leftwards on good holds. This leads to a good belay ledge.

Cwm Silyn Expedition

3. (10m) Now climb directly up for 3m to another big ledge and from this, continue easily upwards again on good holds for another 5m to a huge grassy ledge, known as Sunset Terrace.

4. (15m) Walk left to the end of the ledge. Where it starts to peter out, you'll see a huge pocket, with grass at the bottom. Climb the slabby corner to the left of this and then trend leftwards over a small rib into a groove. Climb the groove, or the ribs either side of it, directly upwards on huge holds. This leads to a good belay in a wonderful position right out on the outside edge of the crag.

5. (25m) Climb the corner above and slightly to the left, moving out onto the outside edge when it becomes easy to do so. Now move up the arete that forms this outside edge to a good belay ledge.

6. (30m) The work's over now; continue easily up the crest of the arete, crossing pinnacles and gendarmes as you go. Many parties will choose to move together on this section but there are plenty of stances if you do decide to pitch it.

Descent To return to the foot of the crag, follow the escarpment edge around to the right to locate the top of a steep and loose chute that descends straight into Cwm Silyn.

To head directly back towards the car, follow the escarpment to the right all the way around the head of the cwm and then walk easily northwest down the gentle grassy slope. As you near the bottom, bear right, back to the path that you walked in on. Follow this over the rusty gate and turn left onto the track.

And now? The options now are rock, or ridge. For rock, return to the crag foot (as above) for another route, such as Ordinary Route (110m Diff), which is slightly easier than Outside Edge but offers fewer memorable positions. For a big and varied day in the mountains put the rope away and pull on your walking boots for a crossing of the splendid Nantlle Ridge – one of the finest ridge walks in the National Park.

Logistics aren't easy. If you are unable to leave a second car at Rhyd Ddu, then you are faced with retracing your steps; a good option in some ways as it's only 4km each way and you can always stash the

Cwm Silyn Expedition

The Pinnacles above Craig yr Ogof Cwm Silyn

climbing gear before setting off. A fit party should easily make the return journey in less than 3 hours. Another possibility is a bus from Rhyd Ddu to Carmarthen and then another to Nebo or Llanllyfni.

Head east from the top of the climb to the 734m summit of Craig Cwm Silyn and then continue north-east from here over Mynydd Tal-y-mignedd and Mynydd Drws-y-coed to Y Garn. There are a few scrambling opportunities (easy Grade 1) at the eastern end.

Mynydd Mawr Expedition

The eye of the scrambler or climber driving north towards Rhyd Ddu cannot fail to be drawn towards Mynydd Mawr, and in particular to the soaring ridges and buttresses of Craig y Bera. The huge screes below the cliffs indicate clearly enough the loose and fragile nature of these unfrequented rocks. Even so, the pinnacled crest of Sentries' Ridge and the continuation rocky ridges above, provide an excellent but serious scrambling route.

Sentries' Ridge, first climbed by Archer Thompson in 1910, follows a

Mynydd Mawr Expedition

well-defined line up a series of narrow ridges and pinnacles just to the right of the large central buttress. Competence in judging rock quality is important, especially when taking a direct line over some of the exposed pinnacles along the very crest of the ridge. On very windy days these are best avoided. However, the most difficult section can be bypassed if necessary, by an escape into a scree gully on the right. The route faces south and dries quickly.

39. Craig y Bera: Sentries' Ridge Grade 3
Vertical height about 150m: guide time about 2 hours

Approach: From the National Park car park at Rhyd Ddu (SH571527) walk along the main road through the village. Just beyond the Cwellyn Arms pub turn sharp left along the road for Nantlle, and then just past a few houses take the forestry road on the right. After about 1km along the forestry track, a waymarked path slants up to the left to a ladder stile on the edge of the recently felled plantation.

Turn right and follow the grassy path along the forest's top edge towards the main ridge of Mynydd Mawr. On the left are fine views down the valley and across to the Nantlle Ridge. Just beyond a stile at the end of the plantation a narrow path contours left to scree slopes below the cliffs. Cross two stiles over a fence and a wall, and pass below

Jerry Rawson climbing the final pinnacle at the top of the Sentries' Ridge

Mynydd Mawr Expedition

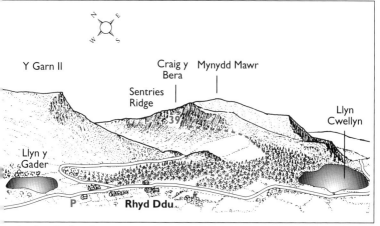

the first broken buttress to a large recess.

The left hand skyline ahead is dominated by a large buttress with a prominent notch about a quarter of the way up and topped by a pinnacled ridge. This is not our route – it is a difficult rock climb. Sentries' Ridge starts at slightly higher level than that large buttress, up the screes to its right, and has scree gullies on either side. Ascend a scree path to the ridge foot.

Start at the lowest rocks of the ridge.
Avoid the short vertical wall at the foot of the ridge by following a faint path up heather slopes on the right, to gain the ridge crest just above it. Climb the next rocks directly or turn them on the right, and then pick a line up the crest of the ridge on heather and rocks. After about 40m of easy scrambling you arrive at the base of some steeper rocks. A direct approach looks quite intimidating, but by scrambling left up broken rocks you can regain the crest about 15m higher.

You have now arrived at the start of the main pinnacled ridge, the exposed crossing of which forms the crux of the route. A rope may be required to safeguard the airy moves over the pinnacles. If you don't fancy this stretch then follow a steep path down to the right into a scree gully, regaining the ridge higher up at a col.

Follow the sharp crest of the pinnacled ridge, which soon leads to an

Mynydd Mawr Expedition

Sentries' Ridge

39

obvious pointed gendarme (rock pinnacle) straddling the ridge and blocking the way ahead. Climb half way up the gendarme on its right side then step awkwardly right onto sloping footholds on a poised block to reach a little notch behind the gendarme. A long sling over the gendarme itself will protect the move. There is some fragile rock here, as can be seen from the fresh scars, and care is needed.

Continue up the ridge over another pinnacle to a broad, grassy col joined by a scree gully coming up from the right where pinnacle-avoiders rejoin the route. This is the end of Sentries' Ridge as originally ascended by Archer Thompson. You have gained about 60m of height at this point.

Ahead is a soaring rocky ridge with steep drops on the left and a faint path up a heather runnel and broken rocks on its right. The ridge looks quite intimidating but its lower section provides some excellent scrambling just left of the heather runnel, to eventually reach another col. Directly uphill from the col, scramble up a ridge to a tunnelled rocky notch. Tackle the steep rocks beyond the notch directly, or avoid them by heather and a rocky runnel on the right. Traverse across the right face of the final pinnacle to reach another heathery col beyond it.

Continue up the last section of ridge over heather and broken rocks until you reach the three final rocky pinnacles. The rock on the first two

Mynydd Mawr Expedition

is shattered so turn them on the left. The final pinnacle is much better and can be climbed directly over its top. A final short section of rocky ridge lands you at a grassy col and heather slopes a short distance below the footpath for Mynydd Mawr. To the west you have a great view across a series of shattered pinnacles and buttresses along the rim of Craig y Bera.

And now? Follow the footpath up the east ridge to the summit of Mynydd Mawr, from where you have excellent views of Snowdon's Cwm Clogwyn and the Nantlle Ridge. To descend return to the top of Craig y Bera then head south-east down the main path around the head of Cwm Planwydd. Follow the steep path down the grassy slopes to rejoin the approach route at the corner of the plantation.

Y Moelwynion

Snowdonia is the only National Park in the country with a hole in. The area centred on the quarrying village of Blaenau Ffestiniog is excluded from the Park, although it boasts a number of attractions from Llechwedd Slate Caverns to the Ffestiniog Railway.

The Moelwynion are actually a small range of rough, rocky hills, but in climbing-speak, 'Going to the Moelwyns' means only one thing: a visit to the collection of crags on the south-east flank of the range, just above Blaenau Ffestiniog. Their reputation speaks of good rock, routes of two or three pitches, and a sunny aspect; it can indeed be dry here when it's raining at Pen y Pass or Ogwen.

But there's more to these crags than just better weather. There's a strong character to the area, its industrial heritage very much in evidence. The little Ffestiniog Railway runs nearby; it may be a tourist attraction now, but its original purpose was to transport slate to Porthmadog.

The three principal crags are Craig y Clipiau, Craig yr Wrysgan and Clogwyn yr Oen. The first two, featured in the Expedition (Routes 42–45), are part of the quarried landscape, while Clogwyn yr Oen has more the feel of a natural crag. Clogwyn yr Oen is in the National Park, as are the main Moelwyn summits, but the excluded area includes all of the ground covered by the Expedition.

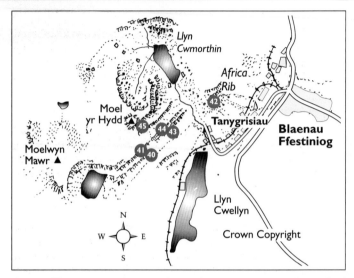

Access: The access is the same for both outings. The most fitting (and most fun) way to arrive is by the Ffestiniog Railway from Porthmadog. Alternatively, the national rail network runs to Blaenau Ffestiniog from Llandudno junction via Betws-y-Coed, with 6 trains daily but none on Sundays. There is also a reasonable bus service from Porthmadog to Blaenau Ffestiniog, except on Sundays. The Ffestiniog Railway can then be used for the last stage from Blaenau to Tanygrisiau, but local buses are cheaper and usually quicker.

Alight at Tanygrisiau and walk up the hill on a road looping round to the right.

By car, from the A496 just south of Blaenau follow signs for Ffestiniog power station; pass Tanygrisiau Station and continue looping round to the right. There's parking indicated on the left, but if you swing right over the bridge then back left and up you'll reach a higher area more favoured by climbers. Thefts from cars have been reported here; arriving by public transport removes this worry.

Amenities

Blaenau Ffestiniog is one of very few towns in Snowdonia that's not

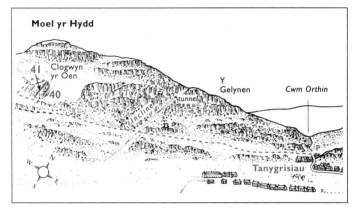

primarily a tourist centre, but nevertheless it has a smattering of hotels, guest houses and B&Bs, as well as pubs, restaurants and takeaways.

For campsites you'll have to head a short distance either north or, preferably, south. In the Porthmadog area, the Eric Jones campsite and bunkhouse directly below the Tremadog crags are run by climbers for climbers. Northwards, another congenial alternative is Dolwyddelan, which has several campsites, a bunkhouse and a choice of pubs.

Clogwyn yr Oen Crag Day

This may only be a half-day for some, but still a thoroughly satisfying one. The two routes described give eight pitches of richly varied climbing, on good rock, with the V. Diff standard well sustained. There's not much between the two routes for quality or difficulty, but it's better to tackle Slick first as it eases you in relatively gently, whereas the opening pitch of Kirkus's is a bit of a shocker when you haven't warmed up!

The approach is by the service road to the dam of Llyn Stwlan, which feeds the hydro power station directly below the crag. The ambience and outlook are less industrial than on the expedition that follows, but nevertheless part of the flavour of climbing here is the background hum of the power station and the occasional tooting and huffing of the trains. The outlook over the lake and rolling hills is very pleasant, with

Clogwyn yr Oen Crag Day

the distant blocks of Trawsfynydd nuclear power station the only blot on the landscape. Though now decommissioned, it is unlikely to be demolished in the foreseeable future, and may well be used for storing nuclear waste until the 22nd Century. And yes, it is in the National Park.

40. Slick 67m V. Diff
Guide time about 1 1/2 hours

A pleasantly varied route, most of it on very good rock. The slab pitch is quite bold and the final crack is strenuous and tricky: the route definitely needs a leader competent at the grade. First climbed in 1953.

Approach: From the lower car-park go straight up the dam service road: from the higher one cross the stream to join it. Craig yr Wrysgan lies just above, and the steep incline at its left end, running up into a tunnel, makes it unmistakable. Follow the road on up for another 600m. Clogwyn yr Oen is the next major crag, just above the road and directly above the power station.

Cross a patch of rushes to a gap in the wall below the left side of the crag. Follow a path up right, just beyond the wall, until the wall levels off. Just above is a large pillar/flake leaning against the crag. Start at the bottom right corner of the pillar/flake.

1. (18m) Climb the front of the pillar, generally keeping right of centre, to a good ledge at its top.

2. (24m) A thin flake stands up at the left end of the ledge. From its top a couple of steep moves lead quickly to easier rock. Go up this for 3m then follow a rising grassy traverse line to the left. At its far end (chockstone runner) step up and then move diagonally right across the wall, below a rowan, to a narrow ledge.

3. (15m - but it feels longer!) Above is a crack formed by the right side of another large leaning flake. Climb the slab on its right, using the edge of the flake at times. Above is a smaller flake, which sounds slightly hollow. From its top there is no more avoiding the issue: step up right and climb a delicate slab, with sparse protection, to a small overlap where the rock changes colour - and the holds improve! Move up to a quartzy

Clogwyn yr Oen Crag Day

Clogwyn yr Oen

40

base of
route 41

spike (treat with respect) then bear left or climb straight up to a good ledge.

4. (10m) The crack above is obvious: how to climb it may not be. Fortunately there's a good chockstone runner (long sling, needed) and jugs aren't that far above. It's possible to belay a couple of metres above the top of this crack, which nervous seconds may appreciate; otherwise continue up the much easier diagonal crack to the top of the crag.

Descent: Go up to the right for a few metres and then follow a well-worn path horizontally left, eventually rising slightly before it reaches a broad open gully which gives an easy descent.

Next: As the gully opens out, bear left, below the crag. Near the bottom is a field of large boulders. A broken stone wall runs over some of these, connecting the wall crossed earlier with the foot of the crag. The broken wall is an exact guide to the start of the next route.

Clogwyn yr Oen

41. Kirkus's Climb 64m V. Diff

Guide time about 1¹/2 hours

Another very good route, with plenty of variety and interest. It is slightly neglected in favour of the neighbouring Kirkus's Climb Direct. The two routes share stances but the climbing is almost entirely independent, and anyone who can climb Severe is recommended to do both. The original and easier line starts with a fierce chimney and continues via grooves and slabs to a delicate exposed slab finale.

The route was first climbed in 1928 by Colin Kirkus, one of the greatest climbers of the 1920s and 30s. Many of his routes, climbed in plimsolls with hemp rope and no protection, still test modern leaders at VS and above, even armed with micro-wires and sticky boots. Famous examples are Great Slab on Cloggy and Mickledore Grooves on Scafell.

Start: Where the broken wall touches the foot of the crag is a steep columnar block, leaning slightly to the left. (Kirkus's Climb Direct starts up the front of this.) Immediately to its left is a deep and usually gloomy V-chimney.

1. (15m) Climb the chimney, which is unwontedly fierce especially for the shorter climber, until it almost closes at the bulge formed by a large block above. Bridge out and use the arete on the right to move up into a notch, beyond which is a little sheltered ledge with a rowan tree. Belay here if concerned about rope drag or if you'd like to provide maximum support to your second on the chimney. Climb the very deep chimney behind the ledge, come out left using the slab on the left, and follow the continuation crack over a jammed flake to a cave-like stance.

2. (12m) Climb the steep crack directly behind the belay. Some classic back and footing helps initially. Thereafter most of the climbing is on the slab just left of the crack. From the top of the slab move right and up, easily, to a large grass terrace.

3. (25m) Above the stance is an obvious arete, split by a shallow groove. Climb the blunt base of the arete for a few metres then move round left into another, larger groove with obvious flaky pocket handholds always coming to light when required. Climb the groove to its top, move left

Clogwyn yr Oen Crag Day

Clogwyn yr Oen

41

Clogwyn yr Oen Crag Day

one metre, then climb a broken crack line with some tufts of heather to reach a small neat stance, the most open on the route but still shielded by a sort of parapet.

4. (12m) A crack used by Kirkus's Direct goes straight up from here: but our route traverses horizontally right from the ledge following a line of small footholds for about 5m. Then follow flaky holds up a slab, trending back left to rejoin the crack of the Direct directly above the stance. Follow the upper part of the crack to a ledge, and move up 4m to a larger ledge with a good belay block right at the back.

Descent: Starting a couple of metres left of the belay block, scramble up to gain an obvious broad open groove running up leftwards at an easy angle. This leads to a grassy bay crossed by a well-marked path. Follow this leftwards to the broad, open descent gully as for Slick.

Moelwyn Expedition
50m Scrambling, 165m climbing; up to V. Diff

The slabby walls of the Moelwynion are incredibly popular as a cragging venue but few people explore the rock that lies above the main buttresses, where short continuation walls offer varied climbing and scrambling all the way to the top of Moel yr Hydd (the hill of the red deer). The climbing is superb; mainly on large and secure holds that follow distinct features and offer great, often exposed positions, high above the valley floor.

With the slate roofs of Blaenau Ffestiniog as a backdrop it's not as glamorous as Ogwen, but the tumbledown mine ruins have a charm of their own, and not many climbing days finish with a subterranean walk-out.

The itinerary describes a warm-up climb on Africa Rib - a classic V. Diff close to the car park - followed by another 105m of quality V. Diff going on the excellent holds and great rock of Lower and Upper Craig yr Wrysgan. From there, a few short steep rock bands offer further sport en route to the grassy summit. With time and energy to spare, a fit party could even pick off Slick or Kirkus's Route on Clogwyn yr Oen (40 and 41, see previous section) on their way back.

Moelwyn Expedition

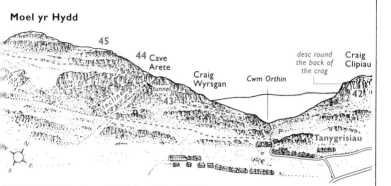

Moel yr Hydd

45

44 Cave Arete

Craig Wyrsgan

Cwm Orthin

desc round the back of the crag

Craig Clipiau

tunnel

Incline

43

42

Tanygrisiau

42. Africa Rib 45m V. Diff
Guide time about 1 hour

An obvious, easy-to-follow line and good clean rock make this an ideal appetiser for a big Moelwyn main course. The quartzy holds on the upper pitches have a sound secure feel to them and the stances are perfectly placed to check out the line for the rest of the day's climbing on the other side of the valley. First climbed in 1953.

Approach from the car park at the road head above Tanygrisiau, via a broad track that heads directly uphill, with the stream on its left. Follow this track for 200m to a pool in the stream. If you choose to miss out the first climb, keep straight ahead here and switch into the description for the approach to Y Gelynen. For Africa Rib, turn very sharp right onto a fainter path that leads up onto an obvious grassy shoulder.

Follow this fainter path onto the first of four slate terraces, and head upwards across a second terrace, and a third one which has an obvious crag on it, to the fourth terrace, where you turn left to the main crag. Continue to some large boulders on your left, and turn right to walk along the foot of the crag for 10m to the bottom of a heathery gully, immediately to the left of a huge sloping overhang. The overhang, which rises up from the floor, is the underside of a huge flake that forms the bottom section of the main rib. About 10 minutes from the car park.

Moelwyn Expedition

Sacks can be left here, as the descent will bring you back past the foot of the crag on the way across the valley to Craig yr Wrysgan.

Start at the foot of the heathery gully, with the overhang above your head to the right.

1. (20m) Move up the gully for a couple of metres and then climb directly onto the face that forms the left-hand side of the aforementioned huge flake (on your right). Keep moving rightwards to some blocks on the prow of the rib immediately above the tip of the huge flake, and then bear left to head directly upwards to a good stance by a solitary rowan tree.

2. (18m) Move left for a couple of steps, back onto the upward continuation of the rib. Immediately above, follow a 3m crack that forms the left-hand edge of a quartzy wall. The angle eases momentarily at a block at the foot of a steep nose. Climb this nose, on good pockety holds that cross another distinctive quartzy section, and continue to a large ledge with plenty of cracks for a belay.

3. (7m) Move right, over blocks, into a corner, and continue steeply up this to the top of the crag.

Descent: For the next climb it'll be necessary to return to the terrace

Moelwyn Expedition

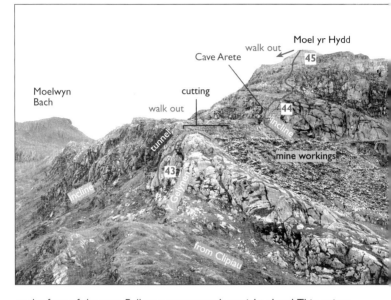

Moel yr Hydd

walk out

Cave Arete

45

Moelwyn
Bach

cutting

walk out

44

incline

tunnel

mine workings

incline

43

Y Gelynen

from Clipiau

at the foot of the crag. Follow a narrow path straight ahead. This swings around to the left slightly, to contour around the top of the hill, then veers sharp right to traverse above steep slabby steps that drop into the descent gully. Continue until you can safely descend into the gully (the further you go, the easier it becomes). Drop down the gully to the terrace at the bottom, and bear left to collect your sack before walking back down the terraces to the main track.

43. Craig yr Wrysgan: Y Gelynen 75m V. Diff
Guide time 1 1/2 hours

Challenging climbing on a steep but slabby rib that offers plenty of reassuring holds but sparse protection, especially on the lower section beneath the holly tree that gives the route its name (Gelynen is holly tree in Welsh). First climbed in 1953.

Approach: Turn right onto the track coming up from the car park and

Moelwyn Expedition

continue away from the car park for a few paces, past the pool in the stream, to a gate on the left. Go through this and follow the path through another gate and across a slate footbridge before continuing through a hole in a wall. Head uphill past a perched boulder on the horizon into a shallow scoop of boulders with a path leading out of its far side. This leads to a very well worn grassy ledge at the foot of the crag. Quartz stripes in the rock at knee level will confirm that you are in the right place. To your left should be a broken overhanging section and to your right, a quartz nose.

Start on this ledge, a few metres to the right of the overhang. The first pitch is little more than a scramble across vegetated ledges.

1. (10m) Scramble diagonally leftwards over heathery ledges to a stance directly above the broken overhangs and beneath a clean rib of rock. You can verify your position by a large grassy terrace that leads off right towards a deep corner. The climb continues up the previously mentioned clean rib of rock that rises just above and to the left of the stance.

2. (25m) Move diagonally leftwards for a couple of metres and then climb the clean rib, passing to the left of a holly tree after 10m and continuing up a finger crack that follows the line of the rib and provides much-needed protection. This leads to a small sloping ledge with a flake that offers good nut placements.

3. (15m) Leave the stance to the right and regain the rib, where after about 6m you have to find your way over an overlap, before continuing easily to a huge grassy terrace (Y Borfa).

4. (25m) Climb the wall on the right of the stance for a couple of metres, and then move leftwards slightly, to follow a series of polished steps in a shallow groove. As this ends, continue easily upwards to the top of the climb. The belays are back a few metres.

Next: Keep ahead and slightly downhill to a flat grassy area and some old mine buildings. Turn left to walk up the incline at the far end of the plateau, with a crag (Upper Craig yr Wrysgan) to your right. Once level with a cave on the right, break right to walk above the cave to the foot of the

Moelwyn Expedition

crag. Follow the crag foot upwards to the base of an obvious arete on the brink of a deep cutting. The climb will follow this arete all the way.

44. Upper Craig yr Wrysgan: Cave Arete 30m V. Diff
Guide time around one hour

This is a great climb that follows a clear line on excellent rock; it's surprising that it doesn't get more use. Huge protruding holds make the first pitch a dream; the second follows the now sharpening arete and offers some wonderful positions.

First climbed in 1967.

Start at the foot of the arete, on the brink of the cutting, just below an ash tree.

1. (10m) Climb the blunt foot of the arete, on climbing-wall style holds, for about 5m to a chimney formed by a flake. Bridge strenuously to overcome this and belay from a good ledge directly above it.

2. (20m) Continue straight up, past the ash tree, and follow the now quite sharp arete to its top.

Next: This is the end of the climbing proper but there's still plenty more rock to play on. So take off the rope but retain the harness. Firstly keep ahead for a few metres to a fence. Cross it, and then follow it up to the left for 50m and round sharp right for a few more paces until you reach the level of the foot of a good crag on your right.

45. Continuation to Moel yr Hydd sections of Diff

Walk along the foot of the crag for 10m to a good arete that forms its right hand edge. Climb this for around 10m at Diff, cross a heathery terrace at the top and then continue up the rock ahead at the same grade – this could all be done in one pitch. Follow the fence for a few more metres up to a sharp left hand bend where you keep straight ahead to another short buttress. Scramble up over the right-hand end of this for a few metres to a good grassy ledge and then continue up a 3m cracked groove at around Diff standard. Nut or sling belays at the top.

Moelwyn Expedition

Now pack away the rope and remove your harness before hopping over the stile above to continue up steep grassy slopes to the summit of Moel yr Hydd.

Next: from here true expeditionaries can advance up the ridge to Moelwyn Mawr and follow a pleasant ridge down to the col to its south; then take a path slanting up and out left to Moelwyn Bach's summit. Return to the Moelwyn col and take a beautifully-built miners' path across the steep east slope of Moelwyn Mawr. This could then be followed to where it meets the path coming down from Moel yr Hydd. The intermittent path can then be followed beneath the escarpment to the mine buildings near Cave Arete. A right turn will lead to the cutting and tunnel described below.

Descent
Drop down to the west, into the saddle between Moel yr Hydd and Moelwyn Mawr, and follow the left hand escarpment edge along to a gate. Go through this and bear left to follow an intermittent path back beneath the craggy escarpment to the mine buildings at the bottom of the incline near Cave Arete. Turn right here and walk down through the cutting and tunnel, before continuing down the incline to its bottom.

Here you could bear right to reach Routes 40 and 41 on Clogwyn yr Oen. Otherwise, bear left onto the main track and then turn left again to return to the car park.

Cyfrwy, Cadair Idris and Llyn y Gadair below

Moelwyn Expedition

Southern Snowdonia

This section comprises three areas: Yr Aran, the Rhinogydd, and Cadair Idris.

The Aran range appears generally smooth and grassy from most directions, but the main ridge carries an extensive fringe of crags on its eastern flank. Its main attraction, however, is the mass of crags in the secluded Cwm Cywarch.

No-one would accuse the Rhinog hills of looking smooth from any angle. They may lack towering monolithic precipices but they have vast amounts of bare rock. The route given here is just one attempt to make sense of this rocky maze, and dedicated explorer-scramblers will find rich pickings.

It seems fitting to end the book on Cadair Idris, a magnificent mountain; more a range than a single peak, and a firm favourite with many discerning walkers and climbers. We have two outings here: one an established favourite, the other a recent discovery that gives a low-grade climb in the glorious setting of Cwm Cau.

Access and Amenities: Dolgellau

The obvious centre for all three areas is the pleasant small town of Dolgellau, nestled under Cadair Idris. It is usually reached by the A470 or A494. There is no direct rail access. The Mid-Wales line (Birmingham - Aberystwyth) passes through Machynlleth, and the Cambrian Coast line through Barmouth; both of these have bus connections to Dolgellau.

Dolgellau has cafes, pubs, small supermarkets and an outdoor gear shop. There are numerous camping and caravan sites nearby.

Near Dolgellau there are youth hostels at Kings (a good base for Cadair Idris), and at Corris, half-way to Machynlleth. A third hostel at Llanbedr is a possible base for the western approach to the Rhinogydd. There is bunkhouse accommodation at Dolgellau Golf Club.

Additional details are given for Aran and the southern side of Cadair under their separate headings below.

Aran

The Aran range runs south from Llyn Tegid (Bala Lake), from where it appears almost as a single peak. The northern half of the range is a single ridge but to the south it divides to enclose the long, quiet Cwm Cywarch. The massive, rambling complex of crags known as Craig Cywarch looms over the head of the cwm.

Access and Amenities

A narrow, dead-end road leads into the cwm. This can be reached from the north (Bala) via Bwlch-y-Groes but is usually approached from the south via the village of Dinas Mawddwy, which is just off the A470 about 15km east of Dolgellau. Dinas Mawddwy is the closest point served by public transport, with 2 or 3 buses daily from Dolgellau or Machynlleth.

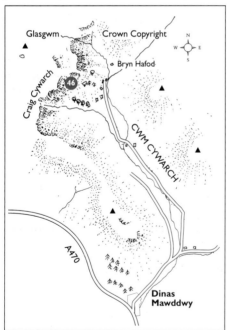

Make sure you catch Service 33 as other buses between the two towns use different routes.

Ideally situated just below the crags is the Mountain Club hut at Bryn Hafod, but it's only open to members of BMC-affiliated clubs, and has to be booked in advance. There are several farmhouse B&Bs on the way into Cwm Cywarch. Dinas Mawddwy has one pub, the Red Lion (Llew Goch), which has home-cooked food, real ale, and reasonably priced rooms. The nearest campsite

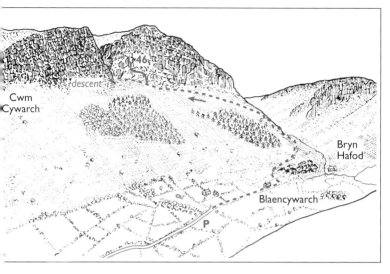

is on the A470 about 1km south of Dinas Mawddwy. Close by is the Buckley Pines Hotel, which has ensuite rooms and serves good food in its bar/bistro and restaurant.

Cwm Cywarch Crag Day

The east-facing Craig Cywarch complex spreads for more than a kilometre. At first sight all appears broken and vegetated, but there are many buttresses of excellent rock lurking in the undergrowth. The most popular route, and deservedly so, is Will-o'-the-Wisp. The approach to the crag is unexpectedly complex and serious and the whole makes for a remarkably satisfying crag day.

46. Will-o'-the-Wisp 95m V. Diff
Guide time about 3 hours

A classic which gives ample reward for the long journey from the main centres. The meat of the route is its third and fourth pitches, a long

Cwm Cywarch Crag Day

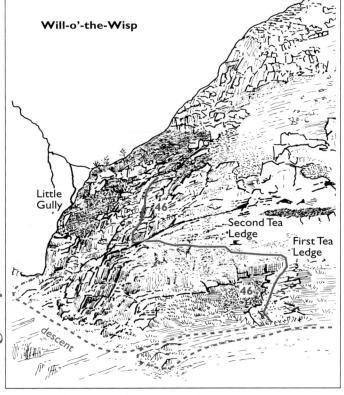

Will-o'-the-Wisp

Little Gully

46

Second Tea Ledge

First Tea Ledge

46

descent

traverse on immaculate rock. That traverse keeps relatively low down, which makes the sudden exposure of Pitch 5 all the more shocking. The traverse itself is well-protected, and the main difficulties are near the end of each pitch, so it is a fairly comfortable route for the second, though complete beginners should still go in the middle of a rope of three - or more. Generous belay-ledges make it a good choice for larger parties.

The route faces east and dries quickly, apart from the first pitch, which is usually wet.

Cwm Cywarch Crag Day

Approach: Cars should be left at The Common, a flat open area across which the road runs dead straight (SH854185). There is a Portaloo at its far end. Park near this, with care to avoid blocking any of the tracks.

Walk on up the lane to its end at Blaencywarch farm. Skirt round to the right of the farm (several footpath signs) and follow the continuation track. It is a good idea to take stock of the crag from this area, which is almost directly below the climb. The easiest landmarks are two plantations below the crag. Above the right edge of the left-hand plantation a large gully splits the crags. This is Little Gully, though it is scarcely smaller than, the next obvious gully to the right, which is Main Gully.

Tap y Graig is the lowest tier of crag between the two gullies. Will o' the Wisp lies here. To the right again, and lower down (roughly level with the top of the plantations) is a broken area of crag, Esgair Felen Isaf.

Leave the track by a stile on the left and follow a good path uphill, heading into the valley to the right of the crags. Continue up this path past some areas of bare rock on the right. Keep going until you can look up to the right of Esgair Felen Isaf and straight up a large gully (right of Main Gully) splitting the main crags. Near some quartz-splashed boulders, the path to the crag forks left off the main path, to climb the bracken-covered slope between bands of scree.

The path may be hard to follow in places, but head up towards the large gully and keep right of Esgair Felen Isaf, then go up left of a much smaller outcrop onto the slope between Esgair Felen Isaf and the main crag. This slope is largely free of bracken and the path is now clearer. Follow it leftward. Care is needed, especially in damp conditions, as there is steep ground and broken crag close below.

Pass below Main Gully and continue until above the southerly plantation. The opening of Little Gully should be apparent just ahead. It is identified conclusively by a wire fence at its foot, with a stile at its right end.. This area makes a good gearing-up point, as there is something approaching level ground and the descent route comes down to here. A sloping terrace begins just to right of the stile, above a low broken band of subsidiary rocks. The terrace extends rightward about 30 metres before it merges back into the main slope – which, at this point, is smooth and grassy, with one isolated block lying directly below.

The lower reaches of the main crag are heavily vegetated, but a band

Cwm Cywarch Crag Day

of cleaner rock cuts up through the greenery above this point.

Start: at the foot of this band, immediately left of a large gorse bush. The rock is clean but often wet.

1. (27m) The band of cleaner rock trends leftward up the initial wall. At the top of the band make a steeper move then step left to a small ledge about 10m above the ground. Move up and right on a vegetated ramp, with more gorse just to the right, then step left onto a short slab. Climb this, followed by steep steps with big flat holds, to a small rock ledge, with deep cracks for belays, below a short bulging wall.

2. (8m) Climb a right-trending ramp below the bulges, to the left end of a long flat ledge, known as the First Tea Ledge.

3. (16m) Step up to a smaller flat ledge. Step up again then traverse horizontally left across a slab which is capped, a few metres higher, by a frieze of heather. The left-hand edge of the slab butts up against a low-relief rib, which runs up to some hanging blocks to left of the heather. Continue traversing to pass around the low-relief rib to gain another short slab; and climb diagonally left up this, quite delicately, to reach another flat ledge. This is - you've guessed it - the Second Tea Ledge. There's a rusty peg belay above the point of arrival, and a slot for a small Friend just above it.

4. (16m) Traverse left along the ledge, and make a delicate stride across a gap to another ledge below a small overhang. Continue horizontally left, with more continuous difficulty, until it is possible to move up a couple of metres to a narrow ledge tucked in cosily beneath a bulge.

5. (9m) Move left along the tapering ledge, then blindly left again round an arete, to discover superb holds on the wall overlooking Little Gully. Move up in a wild position on the right edge of this wall. Protection is hard to find but the holds keep on coming and the steepness soon relents. Belay on a large tree a few metres higher.

6. (18m) Move left and up from the stance to a large block sitting in a corner below a steep wall. Pull awkwardly onto the top of the block

Cwm Cywarch Crag Day

Bernie Carter at the end of the traverses, Pitch 4, Will-o'-the-Wisp
(Route 46), Craig Cwm Cywarch

Cwm Cywarch Crag Day

then climb the short continuation corner on the right to a sloping ledge. Move 2m right, along the ledge, then climb steeply on good holds to another small ledge. The original finish moved left from here, below a sharp-edged flake, to a vertical crack, which used to contain a small tree. The alternative, which now looks more used, is to follow a channel of clean rock up and right; this gives straightforward climbing on big flat holds to a grass ledge with good spike belay above. (For purists who follow the original finish, scramble up and right from the top of the crack to this ledge).

Descent: Scramble up another 8m until a faint path leads off left into a gully (a branch of Little Gully). Descend this on steep heather with a few rock steps until it opens into the much larger Little Gully. A rib of rock and heather splits Little Gully and provides the best descent, until about 15m above the foot of the crag. Move left (facing out) into the gully and descend to the wire fence.

Yr Rhinogydd

The Rhinogydd punch well above their weight. They aren't high but they are the roughest hills in Wales, a tumbled mix of rock and heather, with a few lurking bogs to complete the equation. The heather is remarkably luxuriant and masks treacherous boulder-fields. Away from the paths, going is slow and arduous. In the Rhinogydd, short-cuts - especially in descent - are a bad idea.

Access and Amenities

The route on Rhinog Fawr can be approached from the A470 to the east, which is the more convenient; or from the coast, which is prettier. For the eastern approach, Dolgellau (see the head of the section) is a useful base. Bus services 32 / 35 / X32 between Blaenau Ffestiniog and Dolgellau run along the A470. There's an attractive campsite with very basic facilities at Cae Gwyn (SH714298) and you can walk to the route from there. The nearest pub is the Rhiw Goch Inn, attached to the Trawsfynydd Holiday Village.

The western approach, by Cwm Nantcol, allows you to start off from any of the coastal villages served by the Cambrian Coastal Railway and

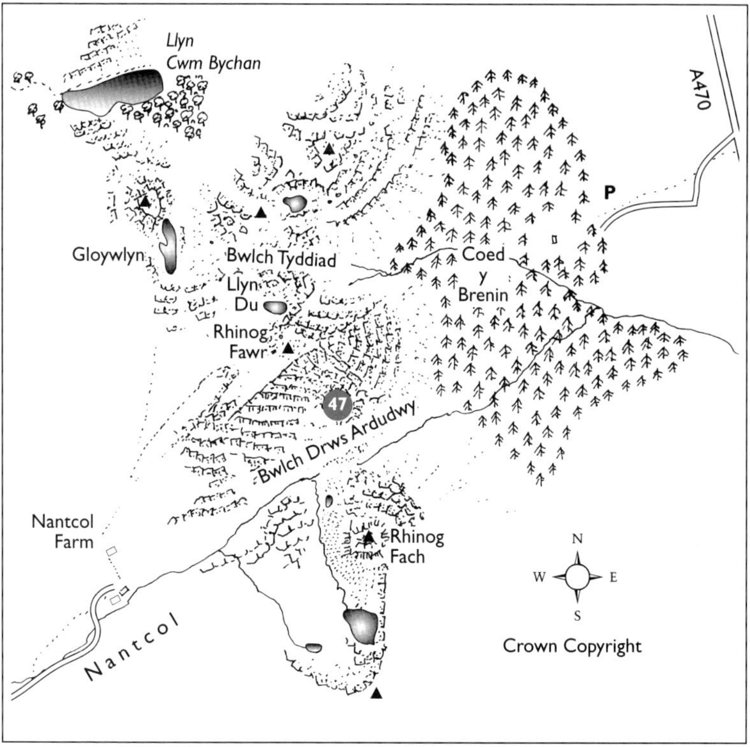

Llyn
Cwm Bychan

Gloywlyn

Bwlch Tyddiad

Llyn
Du

Rhinog
Fawr

Coed
y
Brenin

P

A470

47

Bwlch Drws Ardudwy

Nantcol
Farm

Rhinog
Fach

Nantcol

N
W E
S

Crown Copyright

the No 38 bus Barmouth to Blaenau. Llanbedr has its youth hostel (open late March to early November) and two old inns, the Victoria and the Ty Mawr Hotel. The coast is more for caravans, but there's hillside camping (SH611292) up-valley towards Cwm Bychan, and riverside sites at Tal-y-Bont; Harlech with its justly famous castle has the Lion Inn.

Rhinog Fawr Expedition

One might expect this abundance of bare rock to have been picked over by climbers for generations. In fact there was little development until the mid-1990's, when an intensive period of exploration began. This

Rhinog Fawr

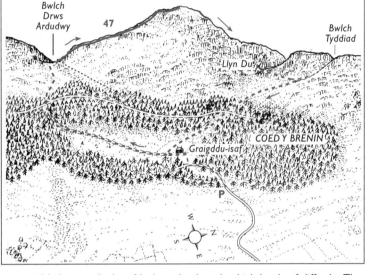

yielded many climbs of high quality but also high levels of difficulty. The bands of gritstone which give the hillsides their tiered appearance are short but steep, and most of the climbs which have been made are in the Extreme grades.

47 Rhinog Fawr Grade 3 but with much scope for variation.
Vertical height about 350m of which scrambling 150m. Guide time about 1 1/2 hours from bwlch to fore-summit

Rhinog Fawr bristles with crags, yet finding a good scrambling line is far from easy, entailing a search for the elusive happy medium between, on the one hand, rock that's clean and sound but excessively steep, and on the other, rock that's just too broken or vegetated to be enjoyable. This route above Bwlch Drws Ardudwy makes a stab at it, and also offers a real sense of exploration.

There are two main sections of scrambling. The first weaves through

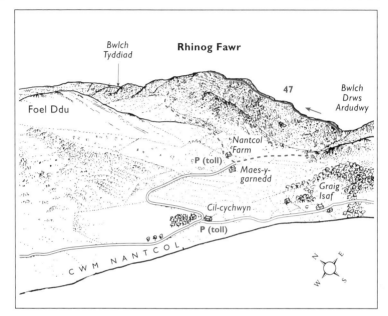

steep crags above the bwlch; the second climbs the face directly below a subsidiary summit - hereafter called the fore-summit. In between is a rocky walk. There are many alternatives, especially on the upper face. The good scrambling is sporadic, but some of it is very good. However the real reward is in the puzzling out of the route and the wild, empty beauty of the surroundings.

Approach from the east is by a narrow gated lane that leaves the A470 at SH713305. The junction is unsigned and easily missed, especially as it lies on a long straight stretch where the traffic is travelling fast. Buses pass the lane end, if you can explain to the driver where you need to get off (Services 32 / 35 / X32 between Blaenau Ffestiniog and Dolgellau).

Follow the lane for about 3km to parking places just inside a forest. Walk down the left-hand track, and where this bends left continue ahead on a muddy path (bridleway) to meet another track by Graigddu-isaf farm. Turn left and follow forest tracks for about 2km, keeping

Rhinog Fawr

3rd Tier

2nd Tier

1st Tier

47

Bwlch Drws Ardudwy

Rhinog Fawr Expedition

straight ahead at each junction; between whiles the route gradually curves round to the right, from almost due south to west-south-west. Where the track abruptly changes direction an obvious muddy path continues ahead. This soon leads out to open moorland with Rhinog Fawr rising ahead and Rhinog Fach to its left. The deep gap between them is Bwlch Drws Ardudwy.

Follow the path across the moor towards the bwlch. A large cairn marks the highest point of the path, but continue for about 300m to the narrowest part of the pass.

Approach from the west: Those based on the coast between Barmouth and Harlech will find the western approach easier. Follow tortuous gated lanes into Cwm Nantcol; park at the end of the lane and pay at the farm. A beautiful path with lots of stepping stones leads to Bwlch Drws-Ardudwy in about 2km.

Start in the narrowest part of the pass, about 300m west of its summit. A substantial wall runs close to the path, and the remains of a small sheepfold mark the spot exactly. Traces of a very ruinous wall, almost lost in heather, run up the slope towards the crags.

Rhinog Fawr

47

Walk up on top of the ruined wall until it gets lost in the heather and boulders. Continue up the slope, trending slightly left, aiming for the left side of the first tier of crags. The boulders make for better going than the heather, and some of them are large enough to give micro-scrambles. A van-size block sits on the easier-angled slope just below the crag. You can aim for this, and another micro-scramble, or by-pass it to its left.

Work left across the boulder-field to the left end of the crag. At about head-height is a large ledge littered with blocks. Get onto this at its left side and follow it to the right. As the ledge narrows the way is almost blocked by a leaning block. Pass behind the block, then climb a short

Rhinog Fawr Expedition

crack below a jutting overhang to gain a higher ledge. Keep moving to the right along this ledge until the steep rock relents. Another slope of boulders and heather leads up to the next band of crag.

The best landmark here is a large patch of ivy in the middle of a steep wall. 10m to right of this at the same level is a substantial tree. Below the tree is the start of a diagonal break running up to the right in a series of large ledges and steps.

The steep clean rock to the right of the break will be tempting to bold scramblers and those equipped with rope, runners and plenty of time. However even the break is not the soft option it may appear, with some awkward moves over the steps, especially the first one.

Follow the break until it opens out onto another rough slope below a third tier of crag. This crag is split by a dank gully just to left of its highest section. Climb the steep stepped rock immediately to right of the gully to a broad ledge at about half-height. Follow this ledge rightwards below a steep wall. Where the steep wall ends, move up a few metres to a higher ledge. Sidle to the right along this until it ends below a recess; then climb the slab just to right of the recess. At its top, level ground awaits.

You can now survey the rest of the route. The ground ahead rises gently, with great sweeps of bare rock, while the fore-summit rises away to the left. Don't make a bee-line for it, as this leads to an annoying loss of height. Instead, follow the trend of the bare rock slabs. These slowly curve left and gather towards a rocky knoll which is the first real rise on the way to the fore-summit. If you want to maximise the scrambling, seek out some rock ribs which extend left from the knoll.

From the top of the knoll, the ground dips ahead, then rises sharply in an unappealing slope of scree, broken rock and heather. A faint path can be found climbing this slope by way of the largest patch of vegetation.

At the top of the slope the final rise to the fore-summit looms ahead. There are extensive areas of boulders and heather but also plenty of good rock. Falling from a notch in the skyline is an obvious gully. Its continuity is broken by a large boulder-field which stretches across much of the face just above half-height, but the gully line is resumed below this.

Innumerable variations are possible on this face. By any line care is needed with the many detached blocks.

Walk up to the base of the lowest of the buttresses, which is

Rhinog Fawr Expedition

Rhinog Fawr's southern face

immediately to left of the gully. This boasts a fairly clear-cut arete between the front face and the short gully wall; the direct ascent of this is clearly the most aesthetic line, but is probably Diff standard. Instead start about 8m left of the arete, and weave up the front face using flakes and heather ledges to a boulder-strewn terrace.

The gully edge of the next tier looks rickety in the extreme, so keep about 10m to left of it. A needle-like flake at the base of the rock points the way. Climb up just left of this needle, using a broader block. Directly above is a heather recess, so move to the right above the needle and climb short corners and cracks to a heathery terrace.

A broad slab a few metres left of the gully is the best line on the next tier. Just above is the large boulder field that breaks the gully line. Pick a careful path up this to an area of heather below the resumption of the gully.

It's possible to continue directly upwards, but the most attractive rock now lies to right of the gully. Go up into the gully until just below a pronounced narrowing, then walk out to the right on a heathery ledge below a broad slabby wall. Near the left side of this wall there's a bold

Rhinog Fawr Expedition

line up left-pointing flakes, or easier options further right, starting over stacked boulders to get onto the right side of the slabby wall.

There's another mass of stacked blocks above the right side of the slabby wall. Skirt the blocks to their left and climb the final tier above by a choice of cracks and corners. The slope above leads quickly to the fore-summit.

And Now? Follow the ridge west for about 500m, across a slight dip, to the summit of Rhinog Fawr.

To return to the forest car-park descend a rough path slightly north of west over broken rock before turning right down a bouldery gully that leads to Llyn Du. Go round the east side of Llyn Du to where a narrow path heads down northeast across heather and rock on the east side of the Rhinog's knobbly ridge. This meets the Bwlch Tyddiad path, which descends to the forest. A waymarked path leads back to the car park.

To return to Cwm Nantcol: From Rhinog Fawr's summit a clear path eases across the bilberry and heather of the southwest ridge (a path

Looking east towards the col at Bwlch Drws Ardudwy with the lower crags of Rhinog Fawr on the left skyline

Rhinog Fawr Expedition

marked in black dashes on the OS Explorer map). After scaling a ladder stile in the intake wall at SH651287 the path maintains direction with ladder stiles as required, across heather then rough pastures, to Nantcol Farm. Follow waymarks directing you around the west side of the farm, then follow its drive down to the valley road.

Cadair Idris

Towering above Dolgellau and the meandering Mawddach Estuary, Cadair Idris is much revered amongst the mountain lovers of Wales. So much so that despite being only the principality's 20th highest peak, its

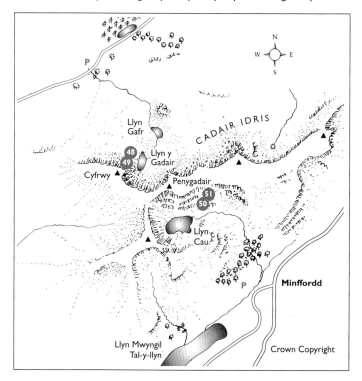

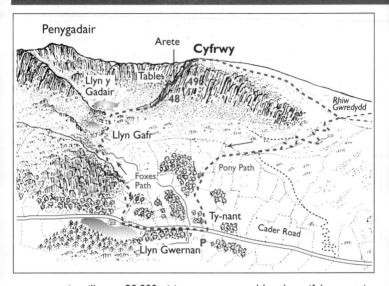

summit still sees 20,000 visitors every year. It's a beautiful mountain, especially viewed from the north, where steep walls of cold grey rock appear impenetrable from the wild moorland below. These cliffs carry many of the best climbs on the mountain. The remainder are found in the dramatic bowl of Cwm Cau on the southern side. Most of the climbs there are in the higher grades, but we have managed to find a thoroughly worthwhile outing in the cwm.

Cyfrwy Expedition
170m climbing, up to V. Diff

Many of the routes in this book claim to be Alpine in nature. But in all Wales, the Cyfrwy Arete really is as close as you're going to get to the real thing. It's made all the more interesting, not to mention 50m longer, by starting out on the excellent Table Direct; graded V. Diff but hardly more difficult than the arete itself. The whole thing can be linked together to provide 200m of top-notch climbing that finishes within a stone's throw of one of Wales's most enticing summits.

On the Cyfrwy Arete

48. Table Direct 47m V. Diff
Guide time about 1 hour and 30 minutes

Easy for the grade, Table Direct slides its way carefully up the steep but-tress beneath the arete using an almost continuous line of distinctive natural features that provide holds, belays and protection. It's often climbed in boots; good practice if you're heading out to the larger ranges, and the angular nature of the generally large holds makes a booted assault only a tad tougher than one using rock shoes. It was first climbed by R.E Davies and H.E. Chatburn in June 1951.

Approach: From the car park near Ty-nant (SH697153), turn left onto the road and walk up to the Gwernan Lake Hotel. Opposite this, go through a kissing gate and follow a path alongside a wall. Once out on the open slopes, the path climbs up to the shores of Llyn Gafr, with great views over towards Mynydd Moel.

Keeping to right of the lake, climb steeply up to Llyn y Gadair, where you fork right off the path to pass to the right of the lake and gain a

Cyfrwy Expedition

Cyfrwy Expedition

small grassy moraine bank that allows good views ahead.

The Cyfrwy Arete is the obvious arete that forms the divide between the main wall running west and the deeply cut cwm that contains the lake.

Make your way up a steep scree path towards the arete but don't go directly to its foot. Instead, keep right, past some tooth-like pinnacles on the right, to reach the crag foot to the right of a huge pinnacle, that is separated from the main face by a steep gully. The top of this gully is marked by another pinnacle, a tall rectangular one that leans on the face itself.

Start immediately to the right of this leaning pinnacle, at the foot of a groove.

1. (22m) Climb the groove, with the pinnacle to the left, to a good ledge. Move easily right on broken ledges, and then, as these peter out, head up diagonally leftwards on small but good holds that lead to a good stance beneath a corner.

2. (15m) Now climb the corner directly, on wonderful holds, to a good ledge above and to the right. There is plenty of protection for a belay on this.

3. (10m) Go to the right hand end of the ledge, overlooking a gully on the right. Climb the wall above, which forms a blunt, leftward trending rib of flaky rock. This leads onto a good ledge at the foot of the Cyfrwy Arete proper.

Next: You are now at the top of the lower buttress, with the complex crag wall of the arete above you. Walk leftwards, along the ledge, with steep rock to your right, and follow it down for a few metres to a groove that splits this face. Facing in, you'll see an easy angled rib that bounds the left-hand side of this groove. This is the start of the arete and has CA scratched into the rock.

49. Cyfrwy Arete 88m Mod, followed by scrambling for 60m
Guide time: 3 hours

Fantastic climbing and exciting scrambling that follow an obvious line and offer all kinds of different situations and positions. Great rock, even

Cyfrwy Expedition

when wet. It's often treated as a scramble throughout, although a rope and some protection would be advisable for the first section and also for the steep wall that climbs above the Table. Moving together for the rest of the route allows fast progress with the ability to build belays as required. For convenience, we have described the whole route in pitches. It was first climbed by O.G. Jones (the 'Only Genuine' Jones, and originator of the Mod-Diff system of grading climbs) in May 1888.

Approach: If not including Table Direct, recce the arete from the moraine above the lake and identify Table Buttress as the rock face that forms the right-hand side of the very foot of the arete. Make your way towards this buttress and then bear left, to flank it via a scree-filled gully. At the top of this gully bear right to join the rocky arete directly above Table Buttress.

Start at the lowest rocks of the blunt, easy-angled Arete, on a trodden stance where 'CA' is scratched onto the rock.

1. (20m) Climb the arete, staying on the crest where possible, until after a short corner the angle eases at the start of a narrow pinnacled section. Belay here, among the pinnacles.

2. (20m) Follow the pinnacled ridge easily and then continue upwards on steep stepped ground to the final pull onto the flat pinnacle top called the Table. There are cracks for protection towards the back of the Table.

3. (5m) Drop from the far edge of the Table into the deep notch beyond. It's a leap of faith with a good ledge for feet, but a nervous second may appreciate being belayed down.

4. (8m) Walk left down the notch for about 5 paces, ignoring a first crack on the right. Climb the second crack, which is well-polished and slopes leftwards up to a large pinnacle at the foot of a steep wall. Belay from the pinnacle.

5. (15m) Climb the steep wall to the right of the pinnacle on good holds and belay from a good ledge at its top.

Cyfrwy Expedition

Awkward descent from the Table on the Cyfrwy Arete

Cyfrwy Expedition

6. (20m) Now continue easily along the arete, which is broad and easy-angled at this stage, until you reach a short steep wall, weakened by a leftwards trending ramp. This is the last obstacle of the route. Either climb straight up the centre of the wall, or follow the ramp up to its top. Belay above.

Next: Continue easily along the arete until it finally spills onto the grassy plateau above, close to the summit of Cyfrwy. Bear left to follow the ridge southeast for 300m, and you'll meet the Pony Path up to the main summit of Penygadair.

And now? The easiest descent is to follow the Pony Path back down to

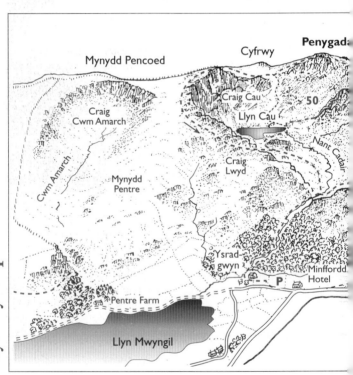

the west and stay with it to cross the moorland below the crags and descend all the way back to road at Ty-nant. Turn right to the car park.

Cadair (South): Access and Amenities

The southern approach, for Cwm Cau, is by the Minffordd path, which starts from a car-park at SH732116, close to the junction of the B4405 and A487. There are two campsites close to Minffordd, and the Minffordd Hotel is right by the start of the Path. Buses between Machynlleth and Dolgellau stop here (catch service 30 or 32 as other buses between the two towns use different routes). There are public toilets at the car-park.

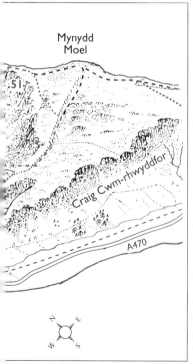

Cwm Cau Expedition

Cwm Cau is Cadair's finest cwm, and one of the best in the country. Above the dark Llyn Cau rises a complex series of crags, culminating in the towering Pencoed Pillar with its monumental right wall. For the competent, the Pencoed Pillar climb, at a worthy Severe grade, is a tremendous outing despite its long vegetated sections. The compelling array of crags in the back of the cwm has led most visitors to overlook the gentler routes that can be found on the sunny flank above the outlet of the llyn.

The route described was climbed in 2004; parts of it may not have been climbed before, though traces of previous travel were found on the easier upper section. The first few pitches offer pleasant slab climbing for

Cwm Cau Expedition

Llyn Cau

which it is well worth bringing the rope. Above this is a rather devious scramble, described as a separate route. Overall this may not be the finest outing in the book, but it does offer some pleasant climbing and scrambling, mostly on good rock, in a sunny situation and with a magnificent outlook. Coupled with the attractive approach, it makes a great way to Cadair's lofty ridge.

The rocks to the right of the lower slabs offer more opportunities for exploration at similar or slightly higher grade. There is further potential for both scrambling and climbing on either side of the upper route.

50. Tapia Llwydion lower slabs 118m Diff, plus walking and scrambling
Guide time 1 1/2 hours

Approach is by the well-trodden Minffordd path. From the car-park follow the signs for 'Cader Idris'. The steepest part of the ascent comes early, climbing through oak woods and past cascades. The path then ascends more gradually as it swings round to head west, into Cwm Cau. After 30 - 40 minutes a fairly level area is reached. A landmark here is a long, low belt of clean slabs to the right of the path; these can case delay if there are keen boulderers in the party.

Here the main path bears left and climbs steeply again towards the ridge enclosing the cwm to the south, while our way bears right just beyond the slabs. Follow a smaller but clear path which runs almost level to cross the outlet stream of Llyn Cau. Directly above the outlet is a broad triangular face of rock and heather, culminating in what appears from the lakeside as a pointed peak. The most obvious feature of the triangle is an area of clean slabs making up its lower left corner; the lower part of these slabs is split into two lobes by a slanting corner.

Follow the path above the lakeshore, and then pant up steep grass to the foot of the lower, left-hand lobe of the slabs.

Start just to right of the bottom of the left hand lobe of the slabs, about 2m higher than the lowest point. A vague groove with some tufts of heather runs up leftwards towards a rounded ledge. Just to the right of the groove foot and a fraction higher up is a vaguely coffin-shaped boulder lying on the ground.

1. (38m) Climb the groove and move along the rounded ledge to its left end. Make a move up into a short crack and climb it. Above this, rather heathery rock is on the left: avoid this by trending slightly rightwards via two short grooves. The angle quickly eases to another sloping ledge.

Directly above now is a parallel-sided groove full of grass and heather. A couple of metres right of this groove, climb straight up over dome-like rock, until the angle eases to walking. Go up to a small patch of grass and heather. Just above the rock steepens again slightly, providing nut and thread belays.

2. (50m) Full 50m rope advised, though pitch could be split at about half-way.

Climb easily up a clean slab to another heather/grass ledge, above which the face steepens up slightly. Climb straight up just to right of a heather-choked crack. The angle eases to another belt of easy slabs. Climb these to their top, to gain sloping ledges just right of a short

Cwm Cau Expedition

steeper dome-like buttress. A nut belay is excavated low on the right-facing flank of the domelike buttress.

3. (12m) Climb the domelike buttress, which eases after about 6m. Walk up grass and heather to the base of the next band of rock. Above on the left is an obvious steep smooth buttress bounded on its right by a wide cleft. The smooth buttress is definitely harder than anything else on the route; so instead climb the narrower knobbly pillar just to right of the cleft. At the top of the pillar is a grassy ramp: move left across this onto an easy slabby rib. Climb this rib to a heathery shoulder.

Walk up a belt of broken heathery slabs and then scramble easily up a broad easy-angled slab. Above this the rock rears up again. There is a broad ledge/terrace below the steeper rock, with traces of a path.

4. (18m) Cross the path and climb two short slabs to reach a flat ledge on the left edge of the buttress, overlooking a stream gully. Above now is a bulbous rocky nose: climb the triangular slab to its right, and emerge onto a near-horizontal spine of rock. Follow its crest until it dips downwards to a slight grassy saddle.

Next: It is possible to finish directly up the hillside from here, with easy scrambling up some broken rock ribs emerging from the hillside. But by traversing rightwards it is possible to continue with more serious scrambling, though it has to be said the rocks are more broken and it is hard to find a consistent line; you either find yourself suddenly on V. Diff rock or have to resort to vegetated scrambling or walking. The line described is easier - in dry conditions - than the preceding pitches and most parties will be happy to scramble unroped.

51. Tapia Llwydion continuation Grade 3
Vertical height about 140 metres: guide time about 1 hour

Approach via the preceding route. Alternatively it is possible to scramble up to the left of the lower slabs.

Start at the grassy saddle at the end of the rocky spine.
Drop down to the right for about 8m, and make an awkward move round the base of the steeper rock above to reach the start of a grassy

Cwm Cau Expedition

ledge running almost horizontally to the right. Follow this until it ends overlooking a broad but ill-defined gully; the gully being more clearly defined lower down. Make an anxious step down into a subsidiary gully, and traverse across it; then scramble up to a little col behind a large spike on a ridge dividing the upper reaches of the broad gully.

Seen from the spike, the ridge which forms the right skyline boasts a steeper lump which, with a little imagination, might be called a gendarme. Move right for about 10m and up about 3m to gain the ridge just below the gendarme. Climb over it or skirt round to its left. If taking the gendarme direct you may want a belay; there's a good small spike at the base of the slab below it.

On reaching its top, the gendarme proves to be all front, with no drop the other side. Above now is an uninviting stretch of broken rock with many loose blocks. Keep to right of this, by going diagonally right up on a grassy ramp with wisps of path. Follow the ramp up to below a dripping black overhang. Continue to right of the overhang up to a short rock rib. To its left is a cave under a boulder, showing signs of occupation by sheep. Climb the rib, which soon peters out into another grass slope. Go up the grass leftward to reach a terrace with several large upstanding blocks.

Just above the blocks is a triangular rock plinth below a bulging boulder. Go up the plinth then where the rock steepens step to the right across grass to the base of the next buttress. Go up this aiming towards a prominent triangle of gently overhanging rock on the skyline. Work round to the left of this triangle and pull out onto the arete about 5m above it. Continue up the easier slab above, to the top of the buttress. Above is a broad open slope, with scattered outcrops. The insatiable can find more scraps of scrambling but it's easy now just to amble up to the main ridge.

Next: As the slope eases bear left and follow the main ridge up to Penygadair, the highest of Cadair Idris's several summits. From here the natural descent is to follow the Minffordd path. This leaves the summit in a south-westerly direction to follow the rim of Cwm Cau, curving round south and then east, finally dropping to rejoin the outward route.

A more direct descent is possible, and may appeal if time or energy are short, or you want to avoid summit crowds. As you come up the slope above the scramble, keep trending right above the last of the crags and

Cwm Cau Expedition

then contour round, below the crest of the main ridge but above the steeper slopes. A narrow but clear path slants off to the right and winds down among broken crags to a stile. A steep direct descent follows until another stile leads back to the Minffordd path just above the woods.

Of course the really thrilling alternative, for those competent at down-climbing, is to continue over Penygadair to Cyfrwy and descend the Cyfrwy Arete (Route 49 in reverse). The line is generally obvious. This gives a day with a real Alpine flavour, though the outlook over Cardigan Bay in evening light is unmistakably, and magically, Welsh.

Also Alpine is the fact that the day ends on the other side of the mountain, a long way from the start. One way to deal with this is to get an early bus from Dolgellau to Minffordd, and then a taxi (possibly at closing time!) from the Gwernan Lake Hotel, which stands temptingly close to the end of the walk-out.

Cwm Cau from Penygadair

Cwm Cau Expedition

What to do when it's raining

A: Go climbing

All the routes in this book, and some much harder ones, can be and have been climbed in the rain. Most of them have also been ascended in full winter ice cover! However climbing in the wet can be disconcerting. You may be fairly experienced on dry rock, but climbing when it's wet or cold sends you back almost to square one.

The best routes for this are where the rock is clean and rough - the ones that would be in the sun if only it wasn't raining! This includes the Tryfan East Face routes as well as Flying Buttress and Clogwyn yr Oen. There are some pointers in the 'Getting Started' section at the beginning of the book about climbing in poor conditions; see especially under 'footwear'. However, if you get too wet and cold you won't function properly or have much fun. Having boots that grip on wet rock is not enough if your hands are too numb to grip. In poor conditions a harder but well-protected route may appear preferable; but, while the leader is happily absorbed in the struggle, the poor second gets damp, frozen and thoroughly fed up - sometimes so much so that it becomes virtually impossible to move, let alone climb. Maybe a scramble, with its potential for continuous movement, is a better bet after all - but with doubled attention to safety.

B: Go to a climbing wall

A climbing wall is no substitute for real climbing, but does allow you to stretch muscles and tendons, and to try technically harder climbs in comfort and safety.

There are several walls in or close to Snowdonia. Most notable is the Beacon Climbing Centre, at Ceunant, roughly midway between Llanberis and Caernarfon. This dedicated centre has several rooms with a total of around 1200 square metres of wall up to 12m high.
Tel 01286 650045: www.beaconclimbing.com

The remaining walls are as follows:
Barmouth Leisure Centre, Barmouth 01341 280111

Bro Ddyfi Leisure Centre, Machynlleth 01654 703300
Dyffryn Conwy Leisure Centre, Llanrwst 01445 712 345
Llandudno Junction Leisure Centre, Conwy 01492 583 592
Plas Menai, Caernarfon 01248 670964
Plas y Brenin, Capel Curig 01690 720214
The Heights, Llanberis 01286 871179
University of Wales Bangor 01248 382571

C: Find a dry crag

It's perfectly possible for it to be raining heavily at Ogwen or Pen y Pass while simultaneously it's quite dry away from the highest peaks. The Moelwyn crags (Routes 40-45) are the most likely in this book to escape in this way.

An even better bet to escape the rain is the collection of dolerite crags at Tremadog, just north of Porthmadog, which lie only a few metres above sea level. There are good bus connections to Caernarfon and Beddgelert, and Porthmadog is on the national rail network. There's a YHA hostel at Tremadog as well as several pubs, and the Eric Jones cafe, campsite and bunkhouse are run by climbers for climbers. These are just a few minutes walk from the main crags, Craig Bwlch y Moch and Craig Pant Ifan, about a kilometre east of the village.

The crags are steep and average around 60m in height. Unfortunately there isn't much choice of routes in the lower grades. There are a couple of scrappy V. Diffs on Craig Bwlch y Moch, close to the cafe, but the best route at this grade is Bramble Buttress on Craig y Gesail, a couple of kilometres west of Tremadog village.

There's better choice for those who can climb Severe, with Christmas Curry on Craig Bwlch y Moch and Poor Man's Peuterey on Craig Pant Ifan being established favourites. Even better is Creag Dhu Wall (the Scottish spelling is correct) on Craig y Castell above Tremadog village, a Hard Severe that features in *Classic Rock*.

The long journey across Anglesey to Holyhead and Holy Island may well be repaid by better weather. The big sea cliffs (collectively known as Gogarth) have nothing below VS, but there are some easier one-pitch routes on Holyhead Mountain. The smaller sea-cliffs at Rhoscolyn are generally steep but there is the superb Symphony Crack, a 20-metre Diff in a beautiful situation. Be careful, however, as the base of the crag is tidal.

D: Go Bouldering

Bouldering is almost a sport in its own right these days, but it has always been enjoyed by climbers as a way to try out moves that they wouldn't dare attempt on a route. Its appeal may be less obvious when everything's dripping, but there's the chance of finding a few metres of dry rock under a sheltering overhang, and bouldering is also a good way to salvage the day when things dry out too late in the afternoon to start a bigger route. One famous venue is the Cromlech Boulders - for access details see Route 28.

Exploring Further

The routes in this book are only the start. There is a wealth of good scrambling and climbing in Snowdonia, and it has been extensively recorded. The books listed below are easily found in outdoor gear shops, especially in the area, but less often in ordinary bookshops. They can also be ordered from their publishers' websites and major online retailers as well as outdoor book specialists Cordee (www.cordee.co.uk).

Scrambles

The original, and still the most comprehensive, record of scrambles in the district is *Scrambles in Snowdonia* by Steve Ashton (2nd edition 1998), though it does not cover the southern half of Snowdonia. It is published by Cicerone Press, www.cicerone.co.uk, ISBN1-85284-088-9

Rock Climbs

The definitive climbing guides to Snowdonia, as well as other areas in Wales and beyond, are produced by The Climbers' Club. The relevant volumes are:

Clogwyn Du'r Arddu by Nick Dixon (April 2004) ISBN 0-901601-73-X
Cwm Silyn by Bob Wightman and Paul Jenkinson (November 2003) ISBN 0-901601-74-8
Llanberis by Iwan Arfon Jones et al. (April 2004) ISBN 0-901601-76-4
Lliwedd by Kevin Neal (1998) ISBN 0-901601-61-6
Meirionnydd by Martin Crocker and others (2002) ISBN 0-901601-63-2
Ogwen & Carneddau Currently out of print These include routes at all grades up to E9, as does *Rock Climbing in Snowdonia* by Paul Williams (1990, reissued 2004 by Frances Lincoln Ltd) ISBN: 0-7112-2408-0.

North Wales Bouldering by Simon John Panton, ISBN 0-954669-70-3 is published by Northern Soul

Recent new routes, and changes to existing routes (e.g. from rockfall) can also be tracked through the following websites:
www.petes-eats.co.uk
www.snowdonia-active.com
www.midwalesclimbing.co.uk

There are few new routes being discovered at the Mod - V. Diff grades, though occasional gems do still come to light. So climbers at these grades can manage very well with earlier guidebooks, which often have the added advantage of being thinner and lighter! However, never forget that routes can change as a result of rockfall or through becoming polished by increasing traffic.

Learning to climb - or learning to climb better
Anyone wanting to learn more about climbing should contact the British Mountaineering Council (BMC). They can advise on training and put you in touch with climbing clubs in your area. Contact them at 177-179 Burton Road, Manchester M20 2BB; Tel: 0870 010 4878; Fax: 0161 445 4500; email: office@thebmc.co.uk; www.thebmc.co.uk

Many outdoor centres and independent mountain guides run introductory and intermediate courses. There are far too many to list here. You could look in the Yellow Pages under 'Outdoor Pursuits', but be prepared to wade through a lot of paintball and quad bike centres! A better bet is to look in the back of any of the main climbing magazines — Climb and Climber — or the more general outdoor titles, TGO, Trail or Outdoor Enthusiast.

The National Mountain Centre at Plas y Brenin, centrally placed in Snowdonia, runs courses specifically for scrambling as well as introductory and more advanced rock climbing. Free brochure on request from Plas y Brenin National Mountain Centre, Capel Curig, Conwy, LL24 OET; Tel: 01690 720214; Fax: 01690 720394; email: info@pyb.co.uk; www.pyb.co.uk

There's no substitute for hands-on experience, but many people have learned to climb safely and well with the help of a good book. A few recommended titles are:
Rock Climbing: Essential Skills & Techniques, by Libby Peter (Mountain Leader Training, 2004) ISBN: 0-9541511-1-9

The Handbook of Climbing, by Alan Fyffe, Iain Peter, Hamish MacInnes (Pelham 1997) ISBN: 0-7207-2054-0

The Beginner's Guide to Rock Climbing, by Malcolm Creasey (Lorenz Books 2000) ISBN: 0-7548-0621-9

The Complete Guide to Rope Techniques, by Nigel Shepherd (Constable Robinson 2002) ISBN: 1-84119-323-2

Visitor Information

Useful websites are:

Snowdonia National Park: www.eryri-npa.co.uk/english/index.php

Wales Tourist Board: www.visitwales.com

North Wales Tourism: www.nwt.co.uk

The following are the principal Tourist Information Centres:

Y Bala
Pensarn Road, Bala LL23 7NH
Tel: 01678 521021
E-mail: bala.tic@gwynedd.gov.uk

Beddgelert
Hebog Centre, Beddgelert, LL55 4YD
Tel: 01766 890615
E-mail: tic.beddgelert@eryri-npa.gov.uk

Bethesda
Fitzpatricks Cafe, 9 Ogwen Terrace, Bethesda, Gwynedd LL57 3AY
Tel: 01248 602416

Betws Y Coed
Royal Oak Stables, Betws Y Coed LL24 0AH
Tel: 01690 710426
E-mail: tic.byc@eryri-npa.gov.uk

Dolgellau
Eldon Square, Dolgellau, LL40 1PU
Tel: 01341 422888
E-mail: tic.dolgellau@eryri-npa.gov.uk

Tourist Information Centres (continued):
  Llanberis
  41b High Street, Llanberis LL55 4UR
  Tel: 01286 870765

  Porthmadog
  High Street, Porthmadog, LL49 9LD
  Tel: 01766 512981
  E-mail: porthmadog.tic@gwynedd.gov.uk

Glossary:
some terms often used in climbing and scrambling

abseil: a method of descending by a (controlled!) slide down a rope. If doubled ropes are used they can be pulled down afterwards. Not to be attempted unless you know exactly what you are doing.

aid: the use of ropes, runners, etc, to help yourself up the climb, rather than just for protection. While the use of aid is a jolly bad show, it is preferable to serious injury or death. However, using aid can sometimes lead you into further difficulties, and it may be better to retreat.

anchor: the actual point of attachment to rock at a belay, or for an abseil.

arete: a sharp rocky ridge, whether horizontal, vertical or in between.

back and foot: a method of climbing a chimney with the back on one wall and the feet on the other.

belay: a multi-purpose word, both noun and verb. It can mean the actual attachment to the rock (the anchor), the act of fixing such an attachment, and the process of managing the rope to protect a partner as they climb. It is also used more loosely to refer to the stance.

bridging: a method of climbing, especially in grooves and corners, with feet spread wide apart on opposing surfaces.

cam, camming device: sophisticated (and expensive) mechanical protection devices. They will fit in parallel-sided and even slightly flared cracks where no ordinary nut is secure. On easier climbs they may be reassuring but are hardly indispensable.

chimney: a fissure in a rock face, wider than a crack but narrower than a gully. More precisely, a chimney is wide enough to get your whole body inside. But if it's too wide to climb by back-and-foot or bridging, it has become a gully.

chockstone: a jammed stone or boulder in a crack, chimney or gully. Can be an aid or an obstacle!

choss, chossy: messy, dirty or loose rock and other debris. Sometimes a general term of disparagement for an undistinguished climb.

crux: the hardest section of a route, usually decisive. Even so, relaxing after the crux is not a good idea!

exposure: in climbing jargon, the presence of a big drop below you. Exposure presents an obvious danger to the unroped, but the roped climber often confronts it in perfect safety - though it can still be scary to those unaccustomed to it.

Friend: a brand (the original, in fact) of camming device, though the term is often used generically.

gangway: a slanting line or upward-sloping ledge on a rock face - but usually one that requires climbing rather than walking. May also be called a ramp.

gardening: in climbing terms, not the cultivation of plant life, but its removal from holds and cracks. For obvious environmental reasons, it should be kept to a minimum.

gendarme: a rock spike protruding above the general line of a ridge, specifically one that presents an obstacle to progress

gill: a steep stream, often with cascades and/or ravine sections, which may be suitable for scrambling (originally a Lake District dialect word, but now used in other areas).

glacis: a very easy-angled area of rock.

hex: (from 'hexentric') a type of nut, usually used in larger sizes.

jam/jamming: a range of methods of wedging fingers, hands, fists, toes, etc in a crack.

jug: (from 'jug-handle') a large, comforting hand-hold.

karabiner (krab): a spring-loaded clip or snap-link, into which the rope can be quickly threaded.

layaway: a climbing technique of leaning sideways away from a hold to maintain balance.

layback: a technique used to climb a crack in a corner, with feet on the wall and hands on the edge of the crack. It's very strenuous and best done quickly. Alternatives such as jamming or bridging are generally preferable.

leader: in rock-climbing, the first person to climb a pitch.

mantelshelf: a climbing move to gain a ledge on a steep wall, by pushing up to a straight-arm position before bringing a foot onto the ledge.

nut: a piece of metal inserted in a crack for a belay or runner.

nuts: common opinion among non-climbers about the mental state of anyone who climbs

peg, piton: a piece of metal with an eye on the end, hammered into a crack. Pegs damage the rock and are rarely used nowadays. Ancient examples may be found occasionally, but may be unsafe. New pegs should not be placed on any of the routes in this book!

pitch: a section of a climb between belays.

ramp: see gangway.

Rock: a brand of nut, though the term is often used generically.

runner, running belay: intermediate protection on a pitch. Mostly for the benefit of the leader, but on diagonal and horizontal sections may also be of great benefit to seconds.

second: the second person in a roped team to climb a pitch. Also, in larger teams, the third, fourth, etc.

slab: an area of rock that's basically flat and is neither vertical nor horizontal; usually considered to cover angles between 30 and 75 degrees. Any steeper and it's a wall.

sling: a closed loop of rope or (more usually) tape, used for belays or runners. Very useful on many easier climbs.

stance: a ledge or other secure place to stop on a rock climb. Normally a place to take a belay at the end of a pitch.

tat: bits of old rope or tape occasionally left on belays or abseil points. May be unsafe and need replacement. Also unsightly and if not necessary should be removed.

thread: a runner or belay formed by threading a sling behind a chockstone or through a natural hole in the rock.

thrutch: an undignified, inelegant and strenuous approach to climbing a crack or chimney. There is normally an alternative!

traverse: a generally horizontal section going across, rather than up, the rockface.

wire: a nut attached to a short length of wire.

Welsh Glossary

Aber	river mouth
Afon	river
Arddu	black height
Bach/fach	small
Bedd	grave
Betws	chapel
Blaen	head of valley
Bont/pont	bridge
Bwlch	pass
Bws	bus
Cae	field
Caer	fort
Carnedd/garnedd	cairn
Capel	chapel
Carreg/garreg	stone
Castell	castle
Cefn	ridge
Cors/gors	bog
Clogwyn	cliff
Coch/goch	red
Coed	wood
Craig	crag
Crib	sharp ridge
Cwm	coomb
Cwn	dog
Dinas	hill fort (or town)
Diolch	thank you
Du/ddu	black
Drum/trum	ridge
Drws	door
Dyffryn	valley
Dwr	water
Eglwys	church
Esgair	ridge
Eryri	eagles abode
Fawr/mawr	large

Felin/melin	mill
Ffordd	road
Ffynnon	spring
Ffridd	enclosed grazing land
Glas/las	blue, green
Gwyn	white
Gwynt	wind
Hafod	high-altitude summer dwelling
Hendre	winter dwelling
Isaf	lower
Llan	church or blessed place
Llwybr Cyhoeddus	public foot-path
Llwyd	grey
Llyn	lake
Maen	stone
Maes	field/meadow
Moch	pig
Moel/foel	featureless hill
Mynydd	mountain
Nant	stream
Ogof	cave
Pant	clearing, hollow
Pen	peak
Person	Parson
Plas	mansion
Pwll	pool
Rhaeadr	waterfall
Rhyd	ford
Saeth(au)	arrow(s)
Troed	foot of
Twll	cavern
Ty	house
Uchaf	high, higher
Waun	moor
Wen	white
Wrach	witch
Y, Yr	the
Ynys	island

Index of Climbs
By Grade

on the Amphitheatre Buttress

Index of Climbs
Alphabetical

Lech Du

Notes

Notes

On the Cyfrwy Arete

Also by Grey Stone Books

Scrambles & Easy Climbs in the Lake District **by Jon Sparks & Judith Brown**
The first volume of the Scrambles and Easy Climbs series takes you on 69 of
Lakeland's best routes. It quicky became a best seller and was highly praised for its
layout and crag diagrams, which, like this book, were drawn by John Gillham.
224 pages
Paperback £9.95   ISBN 0-9515996-4-X

The Famous Highland Drove Walk **by Irvine Butterfield**
Irvine Butterfield, author of the best-selling High Mountains of Britain and Ireland,
takes his readers in the hoofprints of the last cattle drove in 1981, where 29 bul-
locks and a cow called Matilda recreated a journey across the Scottish Highlands,
from the Isle of Skye to the mart at Crieff in Perthshire. In this 128-page book, he
interweaves the story with background history and legend and offers walkers alternative high and low routes. Illustrated with both colour and b&w white photos.
Paperback £9.95   ISBN 0-9515996-5-8

Across Scotland on Foot **by Ronald Turnbull**
Highly acclaimed by the press, this book gives its readers six inspirational coast-to-
coast routes across Scotland, plus ideas and practical advice for planning their own.
An ideal present for both runners and walkers.   160pages
Paperback £5.95   ISBN 0-9515996-4-X

Welsh Three Thousand Foot Challenges **by Roy Clayton and Ronald Turnbull**
This 128-page book is based around the 27-mile Welsh Threethousands route.
While Clayton guides the walkers, Turnbull, an experienced fellrunner, gives the necessary advice for runners and walkers who wish to pick up their pace. The book
includes schedules by record holder Colin Donnelly and former record holder Joss
Naylor, as well as detailed advice on diet and injuries. Turnbull also describes in detail
the 47-top Paddy Buckley round, which can be done as a one-day run (for the elite)
or a 4-day backpack, and the story of near 200-mile Dragon's Back race.
Paperback £5.95   ISBN 0-9515996-6-6

Lakeland Mountain Challenges **by Ronald Turnbull and Roy Clayton**
In the same series as The Welsh Three Thousand Foot Challenges, this book is 160
pages crammed full of information on the Lakeland 3000s, the Old County Tops, the
Bob Graham Round, the Roman Road, Penrith to the Sea and the great horseshoe
walks.
Paperback £6.95   ISBN 0-9515996-8-2

The Bowland Dales Traverse **by John Gillham**
The Bowland-Dales Traverse is a long-distance route spanning 85 miles between
Garstang near Preston to Richmond in Yorkshire, threading through the Forest
of Bowland and the Yorkshire Dales. The pocket book is illustrated by line draw-
ings and black & white photos   64page booklet
Paperback £2.95   ISBN 09515996-2-3-

Long Days in Lakeland by **Ronald Turnbull**
A beautiful coffee-table book that was highly acclaimed by the press. Illustrated with both black and white and colour photos it takes the reader on ten epic Lakeland journeys, including 90-mile high level crossing from Garsdale to the sea and a 95-mile tour of the major lakes. There's also a ten tarns tour and a Scafell Scramble Circuit. For those with less time on their hands, the book also includes ten daywalks and musings on the likes of Borrowdale rain and Ullswater mist.
Hardback **special price** £7.95   ISBN 0-9515996-7-4

Peaks of the Yorkshire Dales by **John Gillham & Phil Iddon**
A popular 128-page book which describes 31 mainly circular walks to the highest peaks in the Yorkshire Dales. The celebrated mountains of Ingleborough and Pen-y-Ghent are featured alongside lesser-known summits. There are 18 full-page colour photos and the maps are 3D panoramas.
Paperback £6.95   ISBN 0-9515996-1-5

See London Walk London by **Nick Channer**
Well-known writer and broadcaster, Nick Channer describes 20 themed walks in one of the World's greatest cities. The themes include 'Government & Empire', 'A Walk with Wren', Royal Reseidences' and "in the steps of Sherlock Holmes'. 160 pages, 8 in full colour.
Paperback £8.95   ISBN 1-902017-00-5

www.grey-stone.co.uk

For trade enquiries please contact our distributors, Cordee, 3a DeMontfort Street, Leicester LE1 7HD. Tel: 0162543579; Fax 01162 471176. Website: www.cordee.co.uk

Jerry Rawson

Jerry Rawson died in August 2009 after a courageous battle with cancer. Jerry was dyed-in-the-wool climber, an excellent photographer, writer, and all-round outdoorsman. One of his proudest achievements was as a founding member of the Buxton Mountain Rescue Team. His essential contribution to this book is just a small part of an outstanding legacy to the outdoors in general.